PAUL CL[…]

Paul Clayton trained as an actor at Manchester Polytechnic School of Theatre during the 1970s. He then worked at most of the country's leading repertory companies, and spent four years with the Royal Shakespeare Company in Stratford and in London.

Television credits include four series of the BAFTA award-winning Channel 4 comedy *Peep Show*, *Him & Her*, *Coronation Street*, *Doctor Who*, *Law & Order*, *My Family*, *One Foot in the Grave*, *Drop the Dead Donkey*, *Doctors*, *Wire in the Blood*, *The Secret of Crickley Hall*. Films include Ken Russell's *Salome's Last Dance*, *The Man Who Cried*, *Ali G Indahouse*, *Fakers* and *Wasteland*.

In 1990 he started a career as a theatre director. He has directed over fifty shows at the Watermill Theatre Newbury, Greenwich Theatre, Nottingham Playhouse, York Theatre Royal and national tours.

He started working in the corporate sector in 1993 as presenter, actor, and lately casting director. This work has taken him all over the world and he has over six hundred corporate events to his credit.

He is an associate artist of the National Youth Theatre for whom he has directed several productions, and he is currently Chair of the Board at The Actors Centre in Covent Garden.

Other titles in this series

SO YOU WANT TO BE AN ACTOR?
Prunella Scales and Timothy West

SO YOU WANT TO GO TO DRAMA SCHOOL?
Helen Freeman

SO YOU WANT TO BE A PLAYWRIGHT?
Tim Fountain

SO YOU WANT TO BE IN MUSICALS?
Ruthie Henshall with Daniel Bowling

SO YOU WANT TO DO A SOLO SHOW?
Gareth Armstrong

SO YOU WANT TO BE A THEATRE DIRECTOR?
Stephen Unwin

SO YOU WANT TO BE A THEATRE PRODUCER?
James Seabright

SO YOU WANT TO BE A TV PRESENTER?
Kathryn Wolfe

SO YOU WANT TO WORK IN THEATRE?
Susan Elkin

SO YOU WANT TO BE
A CORPORATE ACTOR?

Paul Clayton

NICK HERN BOOKS
London
www.nickhernbooks.co.uk

A Nick Hern Book

SO YOU WANT TO BE A CORPORATE ACTOR?
first published in Great Britain in 2013
by Nick Hern Books Limited
The Glasshouse, 49a Goldhawk Road, London W12 8QP

Cover designed by Peter Bennett
Author photo by Craig Sugden

Typeset by Nick Hern Books, London
Printed and bound in Great Britain by
T.J. International, Padstow, Cornwall

A CIP catalogue record for this book
is available from the British Library

ISBN 978 1 84842 281 0

MIX
Paper from
responsible sources
FSC® C013056
FSC
www.fsc.org

For Richard

Contents

Introduction   1

1   Why Work in Corporates?   5

2   From Past to Present   13

3   What's Out There Today... And Where Is It?   23

4   Role-Play... And How to Do It   33

5   Feedback... And How to Give It   67

6   Forum Theatre... And How to Do It   91

7   Live Events... And How to Escape with   115
    Your Dignity Intact

8   Agents, Equity... And Attitudes   149

9   Work... And How to Get It   167

    Appendices
    Survey Results   188
    Companies Mentioned in the Text   194

Introduction

When I'm teaching presentation training on a one-to-one basis to people in the corporate sector, I encourage them to let their audience understand the point of the presentation right at the beginning. If you take someone on a car journey, then they want to know where they're going, so they can sit back and enjoy the trip. It's the same with a presentation: if the audience know where they're going, they will enjoy the journey. And it's the same with this book too. You need to know the benefit of it to you from the start.

For any actor – whether you're an international film star or a jobbing television actor in the UK – a career is about survival and longevity. There are a lucky few who are given a break within the first couple of years of their career, and by further good opportunity and good management, are able to sustain a fulfilling career, doing what they enjoy, and making a good living from it.

When times are trickier, and when there are fewer opportunities, you can do one of two things. You can sit and wait for the phone to ring. If it doesn't, then you can blame this fairly and squarely on your agent. Or you can try and multiply the number of opportunities that may offer themselves to you in any one day. You can cast your net wider. Unemployment has always been an inevitable part of an actor's career. Being prepared for it, and how to deal with it, should be among the skills every actor possesses.

You're a trained professional. You have spent several years learning skills that can be difficult to master, and yet can be useful in so many situations. Suddenly you're deprived of a place to practise them. Work can be easy to find in a coffee bar, a pub, or behind the counter of a shop, yet finding fulfillment for the soul does not come so easily.

In a world where we no longer have a great network of repertory theatres, the opportunities for work for younger actors are just not available. Having worked as a director in drama schools during the 1990s, I can attest that many young and extremely talented people are no longer pursuing acting as a career by the time they reach thirty. Not because their ability has diminished. Sadly the opportunities to fan the flames of their ambition never presented themselves, and they have refocused their energies into another career. They are often aware that it's a second choice. But it pays the bills.

Many actors don't reach their full casting potential until their mid-thirties or early forties. You may be aware that while you'll never be Romeo, you're going to be brilliant as Juliet's dad – if only you're still acting when you're thirty-eight.

This book will show you that there are a whole range of opportunities in the corporate world where your skills as an actor can be integral to the job. Jobs around the world, from Reading to Reykjavik. Jobs where the skills that you have mastered will be a revelation to others. Jobs that will pay the bills. As well as an examination of the work that's available and how to do it well, this book will explain how to get the work in the first place.

Actors learn from other actors – from watching them in rehearsal, and from their anecdotes in the pub. So in this book you will also find tales of personal experience from people who have worked in the corporate market, and how they have made it work for them.

You may find that as you read the book, you decide that corporate acting is not for you. It can be a major mind-switch because the work is all about other people, and not about you. But you may find that using your skills as an actor to help other people in their own personal and professional development is something you find uniquely fulfilling and want to pursue full-time. There are hundreds of actors who now work only in the corporate world, and they do very well. Whatever your choice, you've made the first step towards the next stage of your career by reading this book.

Enjoy the presentation.

Paul Clayton

Thanks

Writing this book has been a huge adventure. As an actor I have always tried to push myself to do new things as a challenge. In taking on these challenges I am nearly always surrounded by a team of supportive and helpful fellow actors, directors and designers, etc., to make sure that the enterprise works.

And so in the writing of this book I have had the great joy, support and words of wisdom of many people.

Thanks to my friends and colleagues, Francesca Ryan and Marianne O'Connor, who were the first people to see the manuscript and whose feedback fulfilled all the rules we will talk about.

To all the people who gave their time for me to interview them: Jillie Bushell, Mark Shillabeer, Janet Rawson, Fergus McLarnon, Daisy Douglas, Jamie Kent, Sally Hindmarch, Tom Eatenton, Marianne O'Connor and Debbie Manship.

To all the people who submitted their stories and their tips about working in the corporate world: Janie Wilson, Robert Shaw Cameron, Andy Spiegel, Toby Sawyer, Elly Brewer, Sian Richardson, Professor Lesley Fallowfield and Janet Ellis.

To Brian Jordan and Kathryn Joekes for use of material.

To Adrian Magson for showing me how I might do it.

To all the clients who over the years have employed me and provided the material and the experience that has made this book possible.

To Nick and Matt and everyone at Nick Hern Books, who guided me on this virgin mission.

And finally to my partner Richard Howle, whose constant belief in me is a joy, and whose gentle inspiration made me get up and write the thing in the first place.

1

Why Work in Corporates?

So what is a corporate actor, and why would you want to be one?

As a small child you didn't decide that you wanted to be a corporate actor. You wanted to be an actor. Perhaps it was because you had taken part in school plays. Or, like me, perhaps you had an unreasoned inner knowledge that the stage or screen was a place you desired to be.

So why would you want to become a corporate actor, a strange, half-life creature that works by day in training rooms and conference centres?

You would not be alone. Thousands of actors across the country derive income from the corporate sector in many forms. But why would you want to join them?

You may have been an actor for several years. The joy of the work is still there, but the gaps between jobs are constantly a problem. These jobs are not what you want to do, and they don't use the skills and experience that you have gained. Ultimately the jobs you do between work can become your life, and can take over. As you have grown older the need for financial stability can change – families, mortgages, the future, etc. The prospect of more regular work can become very attractive, and yet you just can't let go of that bug, that dream that started you on this journey. So often being an actor is just about carrying on. To be able to say in the words of the Sondheim anthem: 'I'm Still Here'.

You may have graduated recently from an excellent course at a top drama school, and yet the work has not come flooding in. You may have had a chance to exercise your skills in theatre or not. You may have done the odd day's television or, if lucky, even more. Yet the main problem can be the time between these jobs. No acting job will ever be permanent or provide any level of security unless you join a soap – and even then, as I know from my own experience, you can be killed off at a moment's notice.

The training at drama school prepares you for being in work. Most training at the major drama schools is based quite rightly around the skills you need to be an actor. Voice, movement, improvisation, stage fighting, and numerous mental and intellectual approaches to the work, such as those of Stanislavsky, Meisner and Brecht. It is all excellent stuff, but you may find you never use it once you have left the training environment. A drama school is a hothouse. It breeds rare flowers. And yet perhaps what is really needed, to continue this somewhat ridiculous gardening metaphor, are hardy perennials. Many drama schools can be guilty of still labouring under the impression that all their graduates will go straight to the stages of the RSC and the National or the Royal Court. Some have branched out and do offer film and television training, but it's never as comprehensive as the stage training and the more general skills they offer.

As far as I know most drama schools offer little or no training for corporate work of any kind.

In coming to write this book, I carried out a small survey. Interestingly only fourteen per cent of people questioned said that their training had included some mention of corporate work, yet in their subsequent careers sixty-two per cent had taken part in some sort of corporate work, be it a live event or training programme.

Many young actors leaving drama schools in the twenty-first century may feel very ill-prepared to work in these environments.

As an actor graduating from a major drama school in the 1970s, it was a foregone conclusion I would go into theatre and so it proved. By the end of my first year out of drama school I had spent eight months working in the theatre, and four days doing television. The following year I went to one theatre for another seven-month period. Repertory theatre work was freely available. Most young actors could be assured of one or more repertory jobs each year. It was where we practised the skills we had acquired and turned them into real, on-the-job experience.

This kind of opportunity is no longer available for most drama-school graduates today. Reps don't produce as much work as they used to. They have to make sure that cast numbers are realistic, and the idea of getting a ten-month contract at a local repertory company to appear in a whole range of plays is an ideal long gone. Figures from Equity show that most young actors work for less than ten days in their first year out of drama school. This means that they do not have the chance to practise their craft. Financial considerations are the most immediate ones. These days there is no 'dole' to support them through the first few difficult months. They have to get out and work. This in turn means they have little time or money to take advantage of places such as The Actors Centre in London's Covent Garden, where workshops for actors to hone and develop professional skills are available throughout the year.

The actor Clive Swift, one of the founders of The Actors Centre, wrote a brilliant book published in the late 1970s entitled *The Job of Acting*, which became required reading for everyone leaving drama school. A wonderfully practical book, it addressed the whole business of treating acting as a job. Running one's life as a business and making it work.

Drama schools offer little or no advice on taxation or saving or mental attitude on coping with no work or on how to survive out there in the real world when not doing Gorky or

Ibsen at the National. The strict financial demands made on young actors these days, which include repayment of student loans, mean that large numbers of graduates are still not making their living from acting by the time they are thirty.

You may now be in that position. Having worked for seven or eight years after graduating, you now feel you need an opportunity to consolidate your abilities and skills as an actor. The constant stream of jobs between acting opportunities can be wearing. It can feel undignified. In my first stint out of work I lasted only one morning as a telesales person, having spent most of the three hours ringing Dial-a-Disc – which just goes to show you how long ago it was – before inventing an imaginary call from an imaginary agent with an imaginary interview for that afternoon. I left at lunchtime and never went back.

As in all areas of life, the people who make a success of the corporate market are the people who apply themselves to it completely. There are now many actors for whom role-play, the most common manifestation of corporate work, is their life. They quite simply don't do anything else, and they take it very seriously.

You will need to find out which area of the corporate sector will work for you. You will need to sort out what your attitude to it is going to be. How you will make it work? Some people I know have taken three months or so out of looking for other work in order to try and establish themselves in the corporate market. They spend this time concentrating on gaining auditions and interviews with role-play and events companies who can provide them with work. It's a little like when actors used to stop doing theatre for a while in order to wait for that nice big television job to come up. Sometimes you're lucky and it does, but in the main you might then be three months further down the line and no better off.

An examination of the corporate market as it exists today will soon reveal something that might interest you. Having decided just what it is you feel suited for, you will then need to gain information on the companies that are providing this sort of work.

Here in the twenty-first century, we have a tool that is unlike anything we have had before. The internet. Whereas finding potential employers in a particular area used to take a copy of *Contacts*, a large pot of coffee and a carefree attitude to the telephone bill, now an extensive amount of research can be done in an hour or so at a computer.

All the companies who provide corporate work for actors have to advertise. They don't advertise for actors. In reality they probably have no shortage of those, but they do advertise for their clients and this will be your first point of access into their world.

You need to set out a plan.

Let's take a look at two case studies of actors who have moved into the corporate market and now make a living out of it. One is my own story and one is the case of an actress who now uses her skills in a new role.

In 1990 I moved from acting to directing my first professional production at the Watermill Theatre in Newbury. Directing was something that I'd always wanted to do, and on the strength of this first production I was asked to do another that Christmas and two further shows in 1991.

This led to an awful lot of people saying to me: 'Oh, you've given it up now. You direct, don't you?' I hadn't given up acting. I had no intention of giving up acting, but I did want to pursue directing alongside it. Two years further down the line I had continued to have success as a director, but no acting work was coming my way, and there was a certain side of my personality that was feeling frustrated. Through friends, I went for an interview with Debbie Manship, who runs the company Role Call. At around the same time I received a letter from Jillie Bushell, who was leaving the production company she worked for to set up her own corporate agency and at that moment happened to be looking for an actor to front a conference for BT Cellnet in Birmingham. She sent me to an audition, and I got the job. This was the first of many corporate appearances. At the same time I went out on a role-play job for Debbie, terrified that I would be found out but keen to try out something new. I wasn't found out, and this led to a whole new stream of work in the role-play world that I was able to pursue alongside the directing work that now mainly occupied my professional life. One of the best things about being a director is that you are in charge of the scheduling. As actors we have to beg for a half-day off, and frequently do, but as directors we can schedule a late start or an early finish to allow us to complete something else. The actors are happy to have shorter hours on a particular day, and the director gets to supplement his small fee with some corporate work.

In 1996 I took over a role in one of my own touring productions, and this led to a renewed interest from casting directors who saw this as my return to acting. It didn't happen instantly, but it was good to know that it might be on the cards. The one thing that remained constant throughout this period was my corporate work. It satisfied the actor side of me. By now I knew several production companies, and producers, who were creating live events that might use actors. Jillie proved invaluable in effecting introductions to production companies using drama in their events.

Alongside this I was able to extend my role-play experience through a variety of corporate clients. I'm not going to say that I wasn't lucky. Lucky in getting the opportunities, but also lucky in the fact that I had the time to apply myself to this work and make it work for me.

Now I balance the corporate jobs with my film and television work. Quite often I give it priority as it's a source of regular income, and loyalty is something that clients do appreciate. I can't pretend that it's never got in the way of my other career as an actor and that occasionally it hasn't been disappointing when I've had to turn down a role or a couple of days' filming on something I would really like to have done because I've already had a piece of corporate work booked into my diary. That's a decision I've made, however. I hope the way I've made it has kept my agent happy, but you certainly have to think about how you run this work alongside the more mainstream jobs you might get as an actor.

A different perspective is given by the story of my good friend and colleague Marianne O'Connor.

❝ I began working as a corporate actor around twelve years ago. The use of actors in training was primarily for assessment centres and to provide business simulations to highlight and explore behavioural impact. I was drawn to the work as it offered a flexible opportunity to pursue acting work whilst developing new skill sets.

Over the years the use of actors in training has developed to include a number of drama-based solutions including Forum Theatre, bespoke role-play and increasingly more work around personal impact and presence, where an actor's ability to marry their drama-skills training to the communication challenges of the business executive are much sought after.

After becoming a mother seven years ago, I decided to focus more on developing my skills in the field of learning and development. I trained as an executive coach. My intention was to have more control over my work/life balance, and whilst I still work as an actor I primarily work as a communication-skills consultant.

I believe my background as an actor has helped to enable my transition into the corporate training world in a number of ways.

I'm an advocate of experiential learning and believe that learning sticks when people are able to put theory into practice. One of the benefits of using actors is in providing the opportunity to play out real-life conversations and situations.

A good business actor is able to assimilate a brief very quickly and ask appropriate questions to convey a truthful portrayal of the character and situation. An actor's abilities to actively listen, observe and understand human behaviours are key to their success in the training and development fields of the corporate world.

As an actor, the casting process requires you to quickly build rapport and leave a favourable and memorable impression. I believe this is a key skill of a good business actor, as corporate jobs necessitate connecting swiftly to a group or individual in an authentic, natural manner.

Two different stories of two different journeys into the corporate world. There is no right way, but there is a way that will work for you. As you read this book, I hope that way will become clear. You can begin to work out how you can move into the corporate world and do the sort of work that you feel you would excel at.

But just what exactly is the 'corporate world' and how did it come about?

Dr Carl Sagan tells us: 'You have to know the past to understand the present', so with that in mind I decided to take a look at how what we know as the corporate market today came into being.

2

From Past to Present

There is a corporate idea out there involving actors that has not yet been thought of. Probably more than one. I'm hoping that your reading of this chapter may be the beginning of that idea. Many of the most prolific and successful companies in the corporate world have been started by ex-performers.

As you work your way through this short history of actors using their abilities in corporate situations, you might come up with that next big corporate idea. History and the past informs us. I remember at drama school spending two and a half hours every Thursday morning doing History of Drama, and indeed taking an exam in it at the end of my first and second years. I may never have yet had a chance to actually use 'cothurni', but knowing that they are the raised boots worn by performers in the Greek theatre has enriched my appreciation of some fantastic designs I've seen in shows over the years and once came in very useful on pub-quiz night.

I suppose it's really hard to decide when actors started using their skills in learning and educational situations for financial gain that wasn't just straightforward theatre. After all, one criterion of all great drama is that it not only entertains us, but that it educates us about the human condition. It's the reason that we can still promote Shakespeare today, for his skill in 'holding a mirror up to nature'.

However, the use of drama specifically as a teaching aid is not new. Way back in Ancient Greece, children learnt through improvisation and dance from the philosopher

Plato. A tenth-century Saxon nun by the name of Hroswitha presented plays that educated her followers on moral issues. And, of course, the actors of the *commedia dell'arte* quite often produced dramas that satirised Italian society of the Middle Ages.

The main thrust of using drama for educational purposes, however, was not really developed until the early twentieth century. US educator John Dewey was a great promoter of 'learning by doing', and drama featured heavily in the theories he applied to elementary schools during the 1920s. Following on from Dewey's work, educationalists across the United States, and later in the UK, developed theatre-in-education techniques for schools, helping children to improve social skills, deal with social issues, and develop their own confidence and self awareness.

In the 1920s, psychodrama was introduced by the psychologist Jacob L. Moreno. He wanted to show that behavioural change in people could be manufactured by the use of various dramatic techniques. He may well have been one of the first people to move into corporate role-play when, in 1933, he led a series of workshops for M. H. Macy, the New York department-store owner, to train employees on customer relations. These are thought to be the first of their kind.

People were keen to make use in their training programmes of the excitement and edge drama brings to audiences. Throughout the 1940s and '50s, role-playing would emerge as a well-used training tool. At this stage the role-playing would mainly be conducted within the group participating in the training. The idea of bringing in professional actors to raise things to a whole other level had not yet been taken on board.

However, as the world plunged into the Second World War, the military weren't quite so slow to realise the value of a little theatrical duplicity.

At the outbreak of World War II, Meyrick Edward Clifton James, a forty-two-year-old Australian-born actor, volunteered his services to the British Army as an entertainer. James hoped for a commission in ENSA, the entertainment arm of the services, but this was not to be. Posted to Leicester, he was commissioned into the Royal Army Pay Corps in 1940. Acting was to be limited to the Pay Corps Drama and Variety Group – until some time in April in 1944, about seven weeks before D-Day, when a British officer noticed that James had a remarkable resemblance to General Montgomery. The officer had seen photographs in a newspaper where James had appeared as Monty in one of those Pay Corps dramas.

Here was a brilliant opportunity to use James's resemblance to the British commander to confuse German intelligence. A young lieutenant-colonel by the name of David Niven, who worked for the Army's film unit at the time, contacted James and asked him to come to London on the pretext of making a film. Operation Copperhead was born. James was assigned to Montgomery's staff to begin copying his speech and mannerisms.

There were several problems. James drank heavily. Montgomery did not drink at all. James also had to give up smoking. Furthermore he had lost a finger on his right hand in the First World War so a prosthetic had to be made.

The main aim of the whole project was to convince German agents that an Allied invasion of southern France would precede the D-Day landings. James was flown from RAF Northolt on board Churchill's private aircraft to a reception at the Governor General's house in Gibraltar, where hints were made about a 'Plan 303' – the plan to invade southern France. He was then flown to Algiers, where he made a round of high-profile public appearances alongside the Allied commander in the Mediterranean. He was then secretly flown to Cairo, where he stayed until the invasion in Normandy was well underway. This high-profile role-play seems to have had the results the Allies required, but for James it brought no success or accolade. Evidently he was hidden away out of sight in a hotel in Algiers with a whisky bottle for company and ended his war still in the Pay Corps having to lie about his five missing weeks. There was no official recognition for his services. The story became a film in 1958, *I Was Monty's Double*, in which James played both himself and Monty. And although it largely follows what is believed were the real events, the story was 'comedically and dramatically heightened' for the cinemagoer's benefit.

I'm not sure how convincing James had to be other than to look like the person he was role-playing, but it's an interesting use of an actor to change people's behaviour. In this case, the whole of the German forces!

At a slight tangent to this, James's story is mirrored by that of a man I met in the mid-'90s. He had started life as a police officer and was placed on a high-level undercover operation to infiltrate a crowd of football hooligans at a south London football club. He lived the role twenty-four hours a day, constantly under fear of discovery, at one point having to lead a charge of hooligans against the police down the Old Kent Road in order to convince his new compatriots that he was genuine. At the end of the operation he was pensioned out of the police force and became... an actor! He enjoyed a good career during the 1990s and has now moved on into property development. Role-play having given him a taste for the real thing, he simply had to try his hand at theatre and cinema for himself.

Post-war and on throughout the 1950s and '60s, many actors found themselves grateful for employment in public-information films. The earliest of these were made during the Second World War and they were made for the cinema. An amateur actor, Richard Massingham, set up a company called Public Relationship Films Ltd and was commissioned by the Ministry of Information to provide short information films on a variety of subjects. These films, funnily enough, often starred Massingham himself.

In 1946, Prime Minister Clement Attlee announced that the wartime Ministry of Information would be closed down. He did, however, realise that official information services still had 'an important and permanent part in the machinery of government' and that 'the public should be adequately informed about the many matters in which government action directly impinges on their daily lives'. To this end he established the Central Office of Information (the COI), which continued to make public information films which were provided to broadcasters throughout the 1960s, '70s and early '80s, free of charge. They were used as fillers for when other broadcast material was unavailable for a particular slot. Actors featuring in them would be paid a one-off fee but could see their work being repeated time after time. This still happens. I made a radio commercial for the COI a couple of years ago for a buyout or one-off fee and it was given an enormous number of airings on London's commercial radio stations. Sadly no repeat fees!

These films warned the public of almost everything from the dangers of playing by a river to the horrors of nuclear attack. They have proved inspirational to a generation of artists and performers. The song 'Charly' by The Prodigy sampled dialogue and the meowing of a cat called Charley in a COI campaign 'Say No to Strangers' that featured on ITV. Urban myth says these feline growls to warn children of 'stranger danger' were voiced by Kenny Everett. Harry Enfield has pastiched these films delighting us with the exploits of Mr Cholmondley-Warner, and yet in their original manifestation they were an important form of communicating with the general public. They often featured actors playing what the writers referred to as 'normal people' – a stereotypical view of the general public – and they are now great works of reference for historians and sociologists exploring society's perception of itself during those times.

The tone of these films was to set strong guidelines for films made by corporate and commercial operations to train their own employees. Training films were very often dull, unimaginative, visual manuals to instruct workers in both process and procedure and made on a shoestring. They were probably often slept through by their audiences, and just treated as a happy excuse for an hour's relief from work.

All that changed with the advent of Video Arts. This industry-leading company was formed in 1972 by Anthony Jay, John Cleese and a number of other television industry professionals. Jay later became extremely well known for writing the hit comedy series, *Yes Minister*, first transmitted in 1980. Cleese at that time was an extremely well-known figure as a member of the Monty Python team but as yet had not produced his hit sitcom, *Fawlty Towers*.

Video Arts intended to produce sales-training films, and indeed that's what they specialised in until 1975 when a branch of Reed Employment asked them if they might make a training film on selection techniques. Up until then Video Arts had not dipped a toe into the management-training market and were surprised to find that it was far bigger than the sales market.

The unique comedy talents of Cleese partnered with Jay's innovative scripts turned Video Arts into a market leader. For the first time these training films were also valid pieces of entertainment. It was easy to see that the 'corrective power of comedy film' was at once a viable training medium. It's still true today. People don't learn when they're asleep, and they learn very little if they are bored. Any presentation, be it video or live, has to interest people and to involve them emotionally if they are to learn from it.

You as an actor are already more than aware of the instant power of comedy. The attention and alertness that a laugh can generate. This is what Video Arts locked in to. Now it's virtually impossible to come across a corporate-training film that doesn't strive to entertain and be amusing. Some fail miserably, but many provide great opportunities for actors to try things out that they might not get in mainstream television.

Owing to the pulling power of John Cleese, the cast lists of Video Arts films read like a who's who of television: Dawn French, Prunella Scales, Hugh Laurie, Robert Hardy, Robert Lindsay and many others have graced their productions. John Cleese sold the company in the 1990s, but Video Arts changed the tone of the training-film market for ever.

We've already seen how forward-thinking the military were during the Second World War in their use of actors. The military had also long used role-play and simulations as part of their training regime. Military exercises designed to reproduce battle conditions are an integral part of training soldiers. It's only a short step from this to actually using soldiers to role-play with each other in such issues as officer and communications training.

The medical profession was not far behind. Though the training of doctors included very little work on communication skills until the late 1970s and early '80s, students would often be required to simulate patients for each other. A surgeon friend of mine told me that, in four years of training to become an orthopaedic surgeon during the 1970s, he had had one single afternoon of communication-skills training. Actors were first brought into medical training situations to pretend to be patients. This was before doctors were encouraged to relate to patients on an emotional level and to create what is now known as a 'patient-centred consultation'. It soon became apparent, however, that the actors brought with them a level of concentration and focus previously unseen in these role-plays, and an ability to convince the doctors about their condition that could take the training to a higher level.

Professor Lesley Fallowfield of the Psychosocial Oncology unit at Sussex University is a fantastic communicator. She has taught me a great deal about feedback skills – you the actor giving positive developmental notes to the person you have role-played with – and the efficacy of good one-to-one direct communication. She told me how she feels using actors has added to her work.

❝ Actors as patient simulators have played an enormously important part in the success of our communication-skills training programmes in the UK. Well-trained actors bring an authenticity to role-play that cannot be created easily by health-care professionals taking the role of patients themselves. Suspension of disbelief that the person one has just had coffee with is now a dying patient is often too difficult for the sceptical trainee and therefore inhibits meaningful engagement with the process and useful learning opportunities. Actors as simulated patients can help circumvent understandable resistance to role-play but they have to be well trained. Although good actors are easy to find, actors who can simultaneously improvise from an outline brief, deliver credible, believable verbal and non-verbal responses to the health-care professional and then provide systematic, constructive feedback following the role-play are like gold dust. I'd like to see the equivalent of Oscars or BAFTA awards for these brilliant people who have contributed so much to medical education, enhancing the communication skills of doctors and nurses for the benefit of patients and their families.

Where the medical profession led, the commercial world followed. Here also role-play was already used as a training method in many workplaces, but people were expected to role-play with each other. The level of concentration and focus that the professional actor could bring had not yet been tapped in to.

Throughout the 1980s and early '90s, a proliferation of role-play companies sprang up. Many of these were run by actors. Actors who perhaps were not getting enough work in the mainstream and who decided to capitalise on the need for actors by businesses, public bodies, and the health service. By the end of the 1990s and on into the first few years of this century, there can't have been many actors who hadn't involved themselves in role-play in some way. Such was the demand that actors were often sent out on jobs with little or no training, and the quality began to suffer. Clients became wary of using actors, some of whom seemed much more concerned with themselves than with the participants they were working with.

This led the role-play companies to adopt strict codes of practice for their actors, and now the top role-play companies, those who get most of the work, have a large pool of actors who focus primarily on this type of employment. This means they are highly skilled. They understand the work environment into which they are about to go, and they treat the job seriously and professionally. It's not just a filler between television jobs. It's a source of income that is keeping them alive. And if done as well as it should be, a source of pride and satisfaction too.

Role-play is now the sector of the corporate world which employs more actors than any other, and we will take a look at it in great detail with a view to making it work for you. You can get an idea of just how many role-play companies are out there by having a quick search on Google, or in *Contacts*, the theatre profession's listings guide published by Spotlight, where role-play companies are now accorded a couple of pages.

Finally in this fast-forward history of corporate work and training, a small footnote brings us full circle. There is one corporate job currently going on that needs very special qualifications. However, before you send in your CV, it's hardly likely that they're going to need a replacement for the current incumbent.

A small, grey-haired, 5'4" woman has been the focus of state events for decades, but pass her on the street and people would never recognise her. Broadcasters obviously need to rehearse many of our great set-piece occasions which involve the Queen. It's a bit of a problem as the Queen doesn't do rehearsals. So the television companies use Ella Slack.

For the last twenty years, this sixty-nine-year-old ex-BBC producer has been in great demand with television companies for lining up shots during rehearsals of such events as Remembrance Sunday, the State Opening of Parliament, and the 2012 London Olympics Opening Ceremony. Not only did she stand in at the rehearsals for the Diamond Jubilee flotilla, but on the day itself, she had a place herself on a boat named, appropriately enough, the Queen Elizabeth.

Using a stand-in allows broadcasters to ensure that the Queen will never be obscured in shots, and allows the Royal Household to make sure that she'll never have the sun in her eyes. She can prove invaluable to all people planning events that might involve the Queen. She walks at a similar pace, which can help with timings. Evidently, Ms Slack doesn't think of it as well-paid corporate job. For her, it's just a bit of a day out.

And it could be for you too. If you're male, in your early sixties, 5'10" tall, weigh in at around 170 pounds and have a slight protuberance in the ear department, then there could be an opening very soon!

3

What's Out There Today...
And Where Is It?

So, having had a look at what has been going on over the last thirty years or so, you will need to look at what's happening now and what's out there for you. Just as you would look through a script to see which roles you might be suitable for, so it would be a good idea to look through the corporate market as it stands today and work out which elements of it would be the best fit for your skills.

Ten years ago, actors were flitting in and out of the corporate market with ease. It was still looked on as something that most actors did alongside their regular film and television work, and in many cases it was something that they didn't mention. Now the situation is rather different.

There are many actors making a very good living within the corporate sector, and some of them don't do any other kind of work at all. They've decided this is where they want to focus their skills. You might ask, as they are no longer acting, how they can continue to call themselves actors. They are using an actor's skills, which they have practised and spent a great deal of time learning, but, by virtue of the fact that they are no longer being employed themselves as actors, are they now in fact trainers, consultants, or whatever other ubiquitous word one might like to use?

To keep active in the world of film, television and theatre and to run a successful and financially rewarding corporate career is not easy but it can be done. You will have to plan it with great care. You will have to develop a sense of organisation about your acting work that perhaps you previously have not had. You will need to run your corporate jobs as a business.

Out there in the corporate market are lots of opportunities for you to begin your business as a corporate actor. Let's take a look at them.

Live Events

The live-events market is huge and as such we will take a much more comprehensive look at it in a later chapter.

You can begin to access what is out there by a simple search on Google. You'll come across murder-mystery evenings, quiz evenings, comedy evenings and dinners. Whatever you come across you can guarantee that it will be the brainchild of an events company.

Many events are thought up as bespoke solutions to a client's problems by the large production companies who manage their conferences and their training weekends. Some of these are what are known as management games. They can involve actors in role or as functionaries to help make the game work. You may find yourself dressed as an Arab sheikh, or modelling a white boiler suit and a huge water pistol in order to pass as a Ghostbuster. I'm not just pulling those out of the hat. They are both things I've done in the past.

In Chapter Seven you will be able to find an in-depth look at the live-events market, what you might be asked to do, and the sort of rates of pay you can expect to achieve.

Jillie Bushell, managing director of Jillie Bushell Associates Ltd, which is probably the busiest and most renowned corporate entertainment agency in the UK as I write, has this to say about actors working in corporate entertainment:

66 The sort of actors who survive best in the corporate entertainment world are those who are quick learners and quick to adapt. Actors can find themselves doing anything from comedy sketches in conferences to being used as link presenters. An actor working in this world needs to be capable of looking after himself. After rehearsal, one of the biggest questions you can often ask is 'Where do I come on from?' You need to think about this yourself and be prepared.

An actor going into a conference or live event for a corporate client should understand the brand. Do a little bit of homework and look up your client on the net. Arrive prepared and be ready to work hard.

Jillie Bushell Associates provide everything to corporate clients, from stilt-walkers, mask performers, and presenters through to major international names headlining the bill. Although they are an agency they don't actually represent actors as such, but they form a vital and integral link between the performer and the corporate client. You can find information about all the companies I mention in this book in a list at the back, including information written by the companies themselves as to how best they like to be contacted and dealt with.

Training and Coaching

Many actors decide to take some form of retraining in order to move into the corporate market and then position themselves as trainers or coaches.

Many presentation trainers are former actors. These are people who work exclusively with clients on the skills involved in making successful presentations at conferences and in meetings at their workplace.

There are also a large number of actors who have retrained as what are now known as 'life coaches', a role where they interact with their clients to provide a sounding board on all sorts of issues, developmental and personal, in and out of the workplace.

There was a time when an awful lot of actors would train as a teacher of English as a foreign language (TEFL) to provide backup income for their acting work. This requires an initial financial investment in completing the course to gain the necessary qualification, and a basic skill in another language to put yourself ahead of the field.

It's perfectly possible to set up as a presentation trainer with no qualifications at all. Presumably it's also possible to set up as a life coach with a similar lack of qualification, but ultimately it's all about finding out how you can sell yourself into the market. Your profile as an actor may help. If you have had success early on in your career and a little bit of a television profile, then people are always interested in meeting 'people off the telly' and that might be the foot in the door that you need.

This is an area where personal contacts will serve you best. You may know people in your own social circle who work in companies where they have to give regular presentations and who may need some help. This sort of corporate work can start small for an actor, on a one-to-one basis with someone you know, and grow on the grounds of reputation and success.

Most of my work as a presentation trainer has been through the recommendation of previous clients, or production companies I have worked with and for whom I have provided the service.

There are a huge number of links thrown up by the internet for coaching and training. I wouldn't begin to know how to assess their worth or credibility. Talk to somebody who has been on the course. Talk to an actor you know who may have made this decision already. Just as you as an actor wouldn't sign with an agency that wants to charge you an up-front fee in order to get you work, so be wary about parting with money for courses that seem to offer work at the end of them. Investigate them thoroughly. Meet the people running the courses, and find out just what accreditation you would have at the end of such a course and how that would help differentiate you from the rest of the market.

Remember, however, that the foremost skills involved in training and coaching are patience and tolerance. While they are both qualities that may be valuable on the film set waiting for the moment when you do your shot, they are not necessarily qualities associated with all actors. You need to ask yourself if you are the sort of person who can work with somebody and put them first at every possible opportunity. Actors who trained in education work, who have run drama workshops, or community projects, can quite often make this shift into the training and coaching world more easily than those who are used to being nearer the centre of attention in a play, television or film project.

Indeed, coaching, and the style of a good coach, is very similar to what you would expect to find in the style of a good director. A person who can enable you to give of your best. Lots of actors are excellent, skilled facilitators because of their self-confidence, but the coach has to be totally focused on the other person. Just like a director they get results by asking the right questions.

'What do you mean by that?'

'What are you saying here?'

By getting people to find the answers to these questions, they move them forward, just as the clever director asks you questions which allows you to move forward in the development of your character

Today, businesses expect coaches to be credited as 'executive' coaches. There are a number of training providers who offer accreditation as an executive coach. Each offers different levels of accreditation from a Coaching Certificate to a Coaching Diploma.

A Certificate would require less coaching evidence than a Diploma, which is more comprehensive and requires more input. For example, a Certificate might only require around thirty hours coaching evidence, whereas a Diploma can ask for up to one hundred hours. The move from actor to coach will take a couple of thousand pounds' investment at the very least. The upside of this is that having a diploma will give you an edge in the marketplace and allow you to charge higher rates.

In the current climate, the demands made on everyone working in the corporate sector are extremely specific. The expectation is that you are much more skilled and the jobs demand more involvement. Actors turning up for a role-play job might also be expected to facilitate. This means that you will run the session and manage the discussion between all the people in the group. Indeed, many role-play companies will show a preference for actors who have facilitation or coaching skills.

Role-play

Of all areas in the corporate market that are available to you for employment, role-play is probably the one you are most likely to have heard of. You may well know an actor who's done some role-play. You might have done a little yourself and be looking to increase your work opportunities in this field.

We'll look at all that later in the book, but to start with let's take a look at the role-play market as it exists today.

There are now a huge number of companies that offer role-play to clients. Many may use different terms on their website to describe what they do: 'business theatre', 'drama-based training', 'theatre play'... However it is phrased, at the centre of this sort of training is the actor's basic ability to bring to life a person within a scenario, and for that scenario to be used in training, development or assessment purposes.

Many of today's leading role-play companies were started by actors. Indeed, you may know some of the leading role-play companies. If not, it's the work of a moment to enter 'role-playing' into Google and to come up with a plethora of references. You may find that some of these references need equipment purchased from Ann Summers and a vivid imagination, but in the main your search will lead you to legitimate companies offering role-play to clients in the business sector.

Let's take a look at two of the companies who are still major players in the role-play market today, both started by actors, and yet both of which are profoundly different in approach.

Role Call was founded by the actress Debbie Manship in 1989. Having had a busy television career throughout the late 1970s and early '80s, she began to find fewer and fewer opportunities for regular work. Debbie learned about role-play from a friend of hers who had just done a small role-play job for Wedgwood. She had the imagination to see the potential, and, together with her good friend and colleague, the actress Sharon Rose, she set up the company initially to provide role-play in medical situations.

Knowing that Charing Cross Hospital were using actors in their student examinations and training, she wrote to them and started work there. She met Professor Lesley Fallowfield, a leading psychosocial oncologist and a sturdy champion of the use of professional actors in medical role-play, and Role Call's profile rapidly increased. At first they tended to specialise in the medical field, but as the company grew, jobs included all the major sectors from the Home Office through to private financial clients, international lawyers, and major retail outlets.

Debbie took over the company full-time in the 1990s, and she continues to run the operation herself. Actors come to her mainly through recommendation, although she does make a point of keeping letters on file and told me that when a job comes in that cannot be filled by her 'regulars', she has been known to ring up actors who she only knows from their letter. She doesn't audition formally as such, preferring to have a quick meeting and conduct a trial role-play with the prospective actor herself.

Janet Rawson is one of the three founders of Steps, which is one of the largest role-play and drama-in-training companies currently in the marketplace. Talk to any role-player and they will have heard of, and very probably worked for, Steps.

Janet and her co-founders, the actors Richard Wilkes and Robbie Swales, founded Steps when Janet and Richard met doing medical role-plays at Guy's Hospital. Their first office was actually the steps of the hospital, where they held their meetings before going into their role-play sessions. It took four or five years for the company to take off, and the three founders had to take a break from their acting careers in order to get the company moving.

As in so many other instances in the corporate sector, it was a practical demonstration of skills that got people interested. A couple of director's chairs, an old chest of drawers and a sad shrub in a plant pot were not the reasons that they won the Best Stand award at their first exhibition. It was the display of role-play that they provided. Showing how much people learn when they are involved.

There's an old proverb attributed to the Chinese that sums up the benefits of learning from role-play:

'Tell me and I'll forget. Show me and I may remember. Involve me and I'll understand.'

How you might get work as an actor in the role-play market we will look at in the last chapter, but it's certainly the area where most actors begin a second life in the corporate world.

Let's assume that's what you've just done. But just exactly how do you do it?

4

Role-play...
And How to Do It

So you've got your first role-play job.

Great.

You are now probably wondering what you might have let yourself in for. What will be asked of you? How do you do the role-play? What types of role-play are there? How do you do the best job possible?

Time to find out.

You have had a conversation with the role-play company. If the job is going to go on for several bookings, you may have had a training day at the role-play company. At the very least you have received a briefing sheet with all the details of the job. But before you get down to studying what the scenarios are and what the information is that you're going to need, it's a good idea to check through all the logistics.

Get Me to the Place On Time

Do you have a venue address? Do you have a telephone number of someone to contact should something happen on the journey? This can quite often be the mobile numbers of your fellow actors, but also it is sometimes useful to have a number for the venue or for the person leading the course.

Double-check the travel arrangements. Many companies insist that you travel on the cheapest possible ticket and that you share taxis to and from the venues with the other actors. It's always a good idea to check this. You don't want to spend money on an expensive rail fare and a taxi to find that you can only claim forty per cent of it back. Check the times of trains for getting to the job. One of the great selling points of actors in the workplace is their punctuality. You know as an actor that being late for rehearsals is one of the few reasons a producer or director can use to fire you. Actors are essentially punctual creatures. This is a great asset out in the wider world.

Take a train that will get you to the venue with time to spare and make sure there is at least one train after that that would also get you there on time. You know from your personal life that railways are not to be trusted.

As well as all your briefing papers, you'll also need a notebook and pen.

And finally the dilemma that can so often face you before any audition or Saturday evening out… what to wear?

Dress the Part

When I was at drama school I heard stories from one of my tutors about how actors were often expected to provide their own wardrobe. In the days of weekly repertory theatre in the 1950s, an actor would have been expected to have a dinner suit, a lounge suit, and one other casual outfit. That is no longer the case, although to judge from the number of jobs, mainly in television, where they ring up and say 'Have you got something you could wear?' those days may be returning. In the corporate world you will be expected to look the part and all the costumes will be coming from your own personal wardrobe.

It's always worth asking the role-play company you are working for what the dress code is if they haven't listed it on the briefing document. The easiest one to follow is 'business smart'. This is suit, shirt and tie, or for females suit with smart blouse. So a suit is a good investment. You can buy a perfectly serviceable one from somewhere such as Marks & Spencer from as little as £70. If you do buy one for your corporate work, I can almost guarantee that one day it'll come in very useful for an interview or audition, so it's money well spent. And, in addition, if you can convince your accountant that you bought the suit purely for role-play work, or for interviews and auditions, then the expense can be claimed against tax.

On some residential courses, which the client may be holding away from their place of work, the dress code is often referred to as 'business casual'. A suit can still work in this dress code, but most often used with an open-neck shirt.

Role-plays in medical situations can demand a less exacting dress code. This is probably the only situation you might get away with jeans, but if in doubt on any job err on the smart side.

Uses of Role-play

As a newcomer to the world of role-play, you will more than likely be sent out by the company you are working for on one of their simpler jobs. It may be to a client's office, or it may be to a residential centre where the participants are taking a course of some sort. Role-play is used in all areas of business these days. The participants – the people on the course you are working with – could be junior doctors, law students, managers in an accountancy firm, debt collectors, doctor's receptionists, or burger flippers. If their communication skills can be subject to improvement, then role-play could be involved. There are two types of situation in which role-play is commonly used. These are a) assessment, and b) training and development.

Assessment role-plays are used in both the private and public sectors. Some of the simplest for new role-players are medically based. These can be aimed at young doctors, training them in communicating news to patients and taking case histories. In the corporate sector, many large law and accountancy firms have assessment centres, which they use for associates wishing to attain partner level. As part of these assessments, a day of exacting role-play scenarios is not an uncommon thing to find.

You could find yourself playing a senior manager making demands on a junior member of staff. You could be someone with poor English in a hospital awaiting test results. You might find yourself trying to get through to the doctor on the telephone and being met with an obstructive receptionist – unrealistic as that may seem – or you could be someone awaiting the results of an Aids test.

In an assessment role-play, your aim as the role-player is to maintain consistency. To make sure that each participant you are role-playing with gets the same level of challenge and that your starting point is the same for each encounter. A popular example of role-play being used in assessment is in patient consultations as part of OSCE exams for the medical students. OSCE stands for Objectively Structured Clinical Examination. All medical students take them. Normally they take place in a large room with lots of different stations around the room. Some of these will have slides, or exhibits for the students to examine. At least five of the stations will have actors and assessors and are known as communication stations. In an OSCE you might be asked to repeat the same role-play between twenty and thirty times a day. Which is why, in order to be fair to the students, it is important to give the same performance each time.

You will have a five-minute consultation with the medical student. You will have been given a scenario, and you will also be given points on which to base the comments you will be asked for at the end of the role-play by the examiner. This feedback, as it is known, should be kept as short and concise as possible. Later you will look in depth at how feedback can be structured to make it work most effectively, but in general, it should be based on what has just happened, and include evidence.

'When he gave me the test results straight away
without any preliminary chatter, it felt very abrupt
and cold.'

You should ensure that the level of challenge is consistent in each role-play. Standardise these role-plays as much as you can. As such you will probably find it helpful to start each role-play in exactly the same way. Find a sentence or a statement that you can believably kick the conversation off with and deliver it with the same tone and inflection for each candidate. After that you're down to reacting. Go where the student's questions take you.

After the role-play, you will be asked to give two marks by the assessor. One mark might be on how the doctor made you feel; the other on how clearly they gave the information. These criteria can vary. Sometimes the examiners will ask for written feedback, but they will not ask you to feed back directly to the student.

This does have the benefit of making these role-plays excellent for actors with little experience in this field. Role-playing in an OSCE is a bit like doing a long run in the theatre, but doing the whole run in a day. OSCEs are great for building powers of concentration. They are also excellent for teaching you not to lead the candidates, but to follow and react.

Later we will look at how to start role-plays, but it's worth bearing in mind that, with assessment role-plays, you are aiming to make them all much the same.

In *training and development role-plays*, your job is to vary the level of challenge according to the objectives of each individual participant. The type of role you might play in a training and development situation will probably be much more varied. You could find yourself being a customer complaining about poor customer service. You could be someone in a team that was being appraised by a manager on their performance. You could be a client whom people are trying to sell to. You might even be someone with a personal-hygiene problem who has to be told that they smell! Some of the roles you might be faced with may strike you as amusing. Be careful. You can almost guarantee that in all cases they will be based on situations that have actually happened. The main difference in these role-plays is that you are in charge of managing the level of challenge you give to each and every participant. You should make sure you respond honestly and authentically to what they're doing. What are they saying to you? How well are they dealing with the issues and challenges in the role-play? There is no point in continuing to be angry, just because that was your brief, if the participant is using effective behaviour to calm you down.

You know as an actor that, in theatre and in front of the camera, no matter how you have rehearsed the line, your delivery of it each and every time you say it should be in response to what has been said before. It's the ideal of acting. It's what we try to achieve every time we go on stage – a fresh and immediate response. You know how difficult it is in a very long run to do this, and yet it's what we strive to achieve. In training and development role-play it's absolutely essential, and yet, if we just listen to what the participant said, it's quite simple. I remember hearing Ralph Richardson interviewed on Michael Parkinson's BBC television show many years ago. Parkinson asked him what was the most difficult thing about acting. Without a second's hesitation, Richardson replied: 'Listening.'

He was absolutely right. It's those moments when you're not speaking, when you have to listen to someone saying a lot of words that you already know, and yet you don't have to just hear them, you have to listen to them. The exciting thing about role-play is that the participants will be saying different things each time. You won't know what is coming up, and you really will have to listen. It's like being in a play where only one person knows the script, and yet, you have to respond to their cues.

Listen to what the participant is saying and react accordingly.

As an actor who spent most of the first fifteen years of his career working in theatre, I know that most of my early television work was absolutely terrible. I didn't really understand the medium and the relationship the actor has with the camera. Once I started doing role-play, where my entire focus was on the person I was doing the role-play with, any thoughts of the audience fell away. This suddenly made me understand how to work for camera. Doing role-play has unquestionably made me a better actor on television. Though there are probably still some people who think I am absolutely terrible!

Types of Role-play

There are two types of simple role-play.

Let's call them 'Pre-briefed' and 'Bespoke'.

You will use the same style of performance and the same feedback skills performing both types. The difference is in how you are given the information to create your character for the role-play scenario.

In the pre-briefed role-play, as the name suggests, the information will be given to you in the form of a written brief before you start the role-play. Bespoke role-play is where you create a brief through questioning the participant just before the scenario is executed.

Pre-briefed role-play

Here you will be given a written brief outlining the scenario. Most often the role-play company sends this to you several days in advance. On rare occasions, you are given the written brief on arrival at the job. A brief can vary from a single side of A4 to a booklet some twenty or thirty pages long. Whatever the size, this will tell you who you are and what the situation is.

Your job is to work through the information and take out what you need in order to be able to play the role.

You can see an example of a role-play brief here. This is a training role-play used with medical students.

Actor Brief

Background

Your name is Philip Williams and you are a successful accountant with a bank in the City. You are married to Fiona, a personal assistant in the same firm. You are financially secure, enjoy an active social life and have recently bought a large house in Surrey. Fiona is expecting your first child in two months' time. You are planning on starting up your own company and have an important meeting coming up soon with your bank manager, to discuss finance for the new venture.

Scenario

You have recently recovered from two attacks of something you have been told is called optic neuritis – you experienced blurring of the vision and pain behind your right eye. This has now cleared up. While you were out jogging about three weeks ago you noticed stiffness in one of your legs, which has persisted to some degree. You feel extremely fatigued at times. Your GP sent you to see a neurologist, who examined you and ordered blood tests, and you had an MRI scan of your head and an 'evoked potential' test (which involved you having lots of electrodes placed on your head). No one has told you what the tests were for; the GP just said they were 'to be on the safe side' (whatever that means).

You are convinced that your symptoms are due to the stress of your proposed business venture and imminent birth of your first child.

[The doctor will tell you that the results of the all tests are consistent with a diagnosis of multiple sclerosis. The doctor is certain of this and must inform you of the diagnosis.]

Reaction

Disbelief – 'The tests must be wrong' – 'I want a second opinion' – 'I've been under a lot of strain lately; probably I just need a rest and good holiday.'

If the doctor is helpful (explains the tests and shows empathy), you start to accept that the diagnosis is correct. In that case, ask specifically 'If it is MS, what is going to happen to me – how's it going to pan out for me?' You can raise the issue of the imminent meeting with the bank and of how this will affect your business plans. Also: how can you tell your wife?

This role-play is used by and copyright of St George's Hospital, London, in Undergraduate Medical Education in a 'Breaking Bad News' teaching context. This sort of brief is excellent for first-time role-players to get to grips with as it is clearly laid out, easy to digest and the objectives for the student doctor and the actor are easy to ascertain.

In this case, as in many pre-briefed role-plays, the student doctors receive their own briefing sheet. It will have less or different information to the one that you have.

You should always read the briefing sheet for the other person in the role-play as well as your own. This is imperative. Sometimes the person who has devised the role-play brief has given the other person extra information that you don't have. Sometimes, and often in error, information between the two different briefs can vary. If not detected early, this can grind the role-play to a halt. More seriously it can undermine the confidence of the person you are role-playing with if they suddenly find the information they have been given is not correct. The brief given to the student doctors that corresponds with the actor brief above is as follows.

Student instructions

You are a Senior House Officer in neurology outpatients.

Philip Williams is an accountant. He is married, and he and his wife are expecting their first child in two months' time.

He has recently recovered from his second attack of optic neuritis in the last few months. Whilst out jogging a few weeks ago, Philip noticed stiffness in one of his legs, which has persisted. He went to see his GP, who referred him to the neurologists, who ordered a battery of tests and investigations.

Results are all consistent with a diagnosis of multiple sclerosis, e.g. visual evoked potentials show a latency delay in both eyes and the MRI shows demyelination. You are certain that Philip has MS and must inform him of this.

Your consultant is at a Trust meeting but will be back in clinic towards the end of the morning and will be able to see Mr Williams if necessary.

Reading the student doctor's brief helps give you context. It provides the story for the person who you will be meeting.

You can see that your brief is really quite easy to understand. You're given all the information you need about who you are. You're given the backstory regarding your visits to the doctor and why you are now seeing the consultant in a hospital. You're also given some possible reactions. These are a real help to a first-time role-player.

When doing this role-play scenario, which I have done many times, it's perfectly fine to choose your reaction before you go into the meeting with the student doctor. The point of this role-play is to evaluate how the student doctor breaks the bad news to you and how he or she deals with your reaction.

Like many things in life, there are three good rules that will help you.

1. *The student doctor should do most of the talking.*

    In any good role-play, it is the person you are working with who should do most of the talking. This may seem hard when you're asked to play an angry patient or someone who talks a lot, but the role-play is for the benefit of the other person, whether they are being assessed or trained, and it's important you give them the chance to speak. I think an ideal balance is at least 60/40 in their favour.

2. *Ask questions.*

    Particularly in a medical role-play, the doctor will be asking you questions. This could mean that you end up doing most of the talking. Try to ask them questions. For example, they may say to you: 'Can you tell me what's been going on and why you're here?' An instant response to this would be 'Don't you know?' If the doctor manages to successfully explain why they need you to give them the case history, it would only be fair to do so. You should always make sure there is a certain level of challenge in the work. At the same time it is your responsibility to guide the role-play to the issue the other person has asked to work on. If they have highlighted a problem with angry patients or people, then it is your job to introduce this as realistically as possible into the scenario.

3. *Don't perform.*

    Some role-plays will take place with you and the
    participant facing each other on two chairs with the
    rest of the group in the same room, possibly arranged
    around you in a semicircle. An audience. Resist the
    temptation that any of your work is for the benefit of
    the audience. The great thing about role-play is that
    everything you do is for the benefit of the other
    person. The great thing about the 'Breaking Bad
    News' role-plays at St George's that we looked at
    earlier is that they all take place in a video room. You
    and the student doctor meet in a private room and
    the rest of the group watch in another room via video
    link. Only after the role-play do you both go into the
    room with the rest of the students. This is great for
    helping you forget the audience and focusing entirely
    on the person who is doing the role-play.

Learning the Brief

You can practise digesting the information in a role-play
brief in the following exercise.

Below is a brief for a business role-play. Read it through and
then note down what you think is essential for playing the
scenario. See how many notes you've taken and then com-
pare it with the preparation card at the end of this chapter.
The idea, of course, is to minimise the information that you
need in order to conduct a successful role-play. Both the
actor's brief and the participant's brief are included.

Case Study 1 – Participant's Brief

You are meeting Robin, who is one of a team of administrators who report to you, their manager. Although the official office hours are 9.30 a.m. – 5.30 p.m., the whole team has been working their own informal 'glide-time' pattern. This has occasionally led to problems when a large workload has been placed on the team late in the day, and there have not been enough staff left in the office to deal with it.

As a result of this, all have recently agreed to come back to their contracted hours, with the exception of Robin who has indicated that he/she wishes to submit a glide-time request to work from 8 a.m. – 4 p.m.

As yet Robin has not submitted an application form for this request, and may be looking for advice. You should explore the full reasons as to why Robin feels that this request is important, and also ensure that you feel there is a valuable business case to put forward for Robin's requested hour.

Case Study 1 – Role-player's Brief

You are Robin. You work as one of a team of administrators providing client services. This can involve updating reports, preparing presentations and general backup and support for the department.

Although the official office hours are 9.30 a.m. – 5.30 p.m., the whole team has been working their own informal 'glide-time' pattern. This has occasionally led to problems when a large workload has been placed on the team late in the day, and there have not been enough staff left in the office to deal with it.

As a result of this, all have recently agreed to come back to their contracted hours, with the exception of yourself who has now submitted a glide-time request to work from 8 a.m. – 4 p.m.

The reason is that you want to feed your horse at the end of the day in daylight.

As yet you have not submitted an application form for this request, and may be looking for advice. You feel there are valid reasons for someone coming in early. Last week a presentation needed updating first thing, and you did it as soon as you got in at 8.00 a.m. You see yourself as being very valuable to the department by providing early-morning cover.

You have got into the habit of leaving at 4.00 p.m., and it is now highly convenient. You can feed the horse in winter months, but in the summer months, this does allow you to get home and deal with your kids, etc., to help out your partner, who also works. The horse gets fed much later in the summer evenings. You do feel that if you had to start staying until 5.30 p.m. regularly, it would create problems such as childcare after school, and missed family time. You may or may not reveal this as part of your reasoning depending on how the meeting goes.

You may be able to accept alternative proposals if you feel that they are suggested as a way forward. You would like some help from your manager with your application for glide time.

Check what you have written with the answer sheet at the end of the chapter. See how concise you can be.

Some role-play briefs can look rather alarming. They can run to many pages. The most frightening document I was ever sent was one from KPMG for a management-assessment day for which the actor's role-play brief was over one hundred and seventy pages.

The same principles apply.

1. Read the entire brief first and then begin to go through it slowly and make notes for yourself.

2. Try and put the brief into a quick précis of no more than one paragraph for yourself and learn that.

3. Write down some likely questions that you might ask. Write out some questions that you think they might ask. (They probably won't ask any question that you write down, but the exercise will help to focus you on the content of the brief.)

4. If you have figures and charts, which you have to know, write them out. You might also copy them out

and have them on your desk in certain situations if this would happen in reality.

5.   Above all, make sure you understand fully what the objectives or learning points of the role-play are. If you're not sure then check with the trainer or facilitator on arrival. This will also help you with your feedback.

You might be wondering about the dubious 'he/she' gender reference to Robin. Role-play briefs are created before the trainers know which actors will be working on them. The characters therefore tend to be given unisex names, so that either an actor or an actress can play them. Chris, Jo, and, at the higher end of the imaginative scale, Charlie, can all feature as popular names for role-play characters.

Curtain Up

Let's get the role-play started.

You've done all the briefing. You're happy with the situation. How do you actually begin?

Remember, the other person taking part in this is not an actor. If the scenario is very clear and they are coming in to you, e.g. a doctor coming into a room to break bad news or do an examination, then clearly it is up to the doctor to instigate the conversation. Nothing more is needed than a friendly 'hello'.

If, however, the situation is a meeting at the table, in front of the rest of the group, the participant may be nervous about starting. If you're sitting down at the table to start the role-play, then it's very helpful if you can instigate the conversation. You might want to introduce some of the quality of your character. For example, a problem worker might sit down opposite their manager with the words: 'You wanted to see me.'

You will really help the other person if you get things started.

Once you've instigated the conversation, however, resist the temptation to start dumping all the information in your brief onto the participant in one go. Listen to what they have to say and then be reactive.

For example, if you're working on a brief with a young doctor, such as the one above, it's not helpful if, when they enter the room, you start off with:

> 'Oh, doctor, it's really good to see you. I was wondering if you had got the results of my test yet because I'm pretty worried about them, although I'm really sure it's nothing serious as my wife is due to have a baby and what with the stress of starting my new business I've been really worried about everything so it would be very helpful if you could tell me that it's nothing to worry about.' (*Take a breath.*)

Not as unrealistic as it might sound. You have spent a lot of time preparing your brief, and you might be nervous. I must have done hundreds of role-plays over the last twenty years, and yet each time I get a new brief I get butterflies in my stomach. I give in to the fear that as soon as I start the scenario all the information will fly out of my brain. Don't worry. It doesn't, and you won't need it all in one go. It's a little like making an entrance in Act One and worrying about your lines in Act Five! You wouldn't do that in the theatre, and you don't have to here. One line at a time.

After that first line all you have to do is listen. The participant, whatever the situation is, will begin to develop it, and that's what you should react to.

If you've been asked to be an angry patient, the first thing they say might absolutely calm you down. It's unlikely, but it has been known to happen.

I once did a demonstration role-play in Monaco. The doctor was a senior cancer specialist, an oncologist very highly respected in her field. I had been briefed to be a very angry patient who refused to accept her diagnosis. As she sat down I snapped at her: 'Come on then, doctor, do your worst.' She took a huge pause, manfully picked up her chair and moved it closer to mine, and placed a caring hand on my forearm. She looked me in the eye and said: 'This is not going to be good news.' Try as I might, this supreme demonstration of empathy and understanding made it extremely difficult to continue at any height of anger. By the time she had delivered the news, I was in tears. It was not what I had set out to do, but it was entirely reactive as to how she had spoken to me. I would like to think my tears were honest and genuine as a result of what she had done.

It still gave plenty of room for feedback and discussion at the end of the role-play as to how she had unwittingly deflected the patient's anger.

Again, relate this to your acting work. You might spend a lot of time on the preparation of a scene or a speech at home. When you take it into rehearsal, however, it changes because of what the other actors you are working with do. It would be wrong to just stay with the performance you rehearsed in isolation.

You may be asked to demonstrate a particular emotion in the role-play – anger, grief, denial. Yet if the person you are working with uses good behaviours, it would be wrong to stay resolutely in that mood just because it's what you've been told to do. As a role-player, you are reactive. You are rewarding the behaviours of the person you are working with.

Your instinct as an actor is to create a scene. To make something happen. Yet, as you probably know and have experienced in your work, some of the very best improvisations are those in which very little happens and things develop slowly. The role-play may seem very dull, but the learning gained from it can be enormous. You need to resist the temptation as an actor to make sure that the scene 'works'. Resist the temptation to push the scenario to a climax. It really isn't needed for it to be a successful role-play.

However, sometimes the behaviour of the participant is so effective that the role-play might be over very quickly. You might need to try and prolong the meeting. You may need to introduce new impetuses in order to challenge them further.

Role-play Techniques

Let's take a look at some techniques that you might use:

Get them talking

In any role-play, the other person should be doing the majority of the talking. It's not an opportunity for you to regurgitate all the facts from the brief. Most role-play situations provide a problem or challenge. In a perfect outcome, the participant will solve this.

You don't want them solving it, however, in thirty seconds.

You might find the use of the non-specific question particularly advantageous. If they've just given you a lot of information, information that you as an actor may or may not understand, then there are ways of responding to move the role-play forward without necessarily having to start regurgitating lots of facts.

Responses such as 'I'm not absolutely clear about that', 'and what would you do?' or a carefully phrased '… And?' will all encourage the participant to give you more information or to make the picture clearer. In moments of utter panic when the other person has just given you a load of information that you really don't understand, you could always try 'just run that by me again'.

How you respond, of course, depends on your character's relationship to the other person. In many instances you will be playing someone who is subordinate to them. In some cases they will be trying to manage upwards, and you will be playing a senior partner or manager. Often in medical role-play, you as the patient can choose your relationship to the doctor.

In all cases, you should be endeavouring to get the other person to do the talking.

Use of silence

This is a particularly good technique, and one that you can also refer back to in your feedback. When asked a question, and in particular a difficult one, don't feel the need to reply immediately. Don't try and cover up. If, despite having read the brief and assimilated as much information as you can, you don't understand the question that has been asked, you can take a good long pause to think about what you might say.

Quite often you will not be allowed to finish this pause. The participant will jump in with another question, most probably simpler, and almost certainly more helpful. This should give you a chance to regroup in the sense of working out what information you now need to share, but also it will become a valuable feedback point for the participant: if they ask a good question, they should be comfortable with silence and wait for the answer.

Performance level

As an actor you are used to performing for an audience. Though entirely within your character, you have an awareness that you are being watched, and it's this that helps you filter where you move on the stage, etc. It allows you the timing you need in comedy. It allows you to keep a stage fight safe, while fully believing that you are trying to harm the person you are attacking.

In role-play, your performance is entirely for the benefit of the person you are role-playing with. The participant.

The set-up may vary depending on the job.

You may be in the same room with all the other people attending that particular course, and you and the participant may be facing each other on two chairs at the front of the room. You may both be in a separate room and your role-play may be being relayed to the rest of the course by means of a video camera. Whatever the situation, you should keep the performance level as real and naturalistic as you can. When you start the role-play try to ensure that you don't begin with an overly loud or large 'hello'. You really want to try to persuade the participant that no 'acting' is going to take place.

Your own internal monitors should ensure that the volume level is audible for the rest of the group (if they are in the rest of the room), but the performance levels should be in no way threatening. It's not about you. It's about them.

Bringing it to a close

You will probably be given a rough idea of the time of the scenario by the facilitator. If not, you can work out the timing that should be allotted to each role-play having divided the number of people in your group by the overall time. Always remember to allow at least as much time for feedback as you have done on the role-play.

Ten minute role-play = ten minute feedback minimum.

You should keep an eye on your watch. If there is no sign that the participant is bringing the meeting to a close, then you should try and introduce something that will allow them to do this.

'Is that everything because I've got to get back to my desk?'

'Really got a lot of work to do this afternoon so if there's nothing more.'

You should guide this gently. You can't make the other person stop and neither should you try. Just use some hints that time is up. Be careful not to offer a solution in order to bring the role-play to a close.

'Oh yes I can hear what you're saying and I'll make sure that I'm not late again and I will immediately try and improve my time management or go on a course to help me cope with prioritising!'

If they are still intent on continuing and hammering home the point, this may be part of the feedback that you will be able to contribute later.

An ideal conclusion would be that you have suggested you have to get back to your desk, and the participant asks you to sum up what has been agreed at the meeting. If you can leave the participant with a feeling of conclusion, then he or she will feel the role-play has been more successful.

This is not always possible, but it is something that you should aim for. It can also help with the delivery of developmental feedback if the participant thinks that at the very least they managed to get through the whole meeting.

All of these performance points are also used in the second type of role-play.

Bespoke Role-play

The good thing about this sort of role-play for you as an actor is that there is no preparation you can do. You are not sent a brief in advance and you have nothing to learn before the job. You just turn up ready to go. Of course, the downside of this is that you won't know what you're in for, and if you are the kind of actor who likes to make choices about things before stepping onto the rehearsal-room floor, then this can be daunting. It can make you feel more nervous. If that's the case, then do a little background reading about the company you will be working for. Look at their website. Don't overcomplicate things, however. The best way is for you to turn up and be prepared to listen to what they ask of you, and go with it.

Bespoke role-play is used mainly on training and development courses where participants want to examine situations that they have faced in the past and feel that they could have achieved a better resolution, or to look at situations or difficult meetings they have facing them in the future. The participant creates a situation. They will tell you whom you will play and working together you agree an objective that the role-play will seek to achieve.

As with pre-briefed role-plays, knowing how the facilitator wants to run the session is vital. It's a good idea to arrive a little early and make contact with the facilitator and have a quick chat as to how they would like the session to run. Often when doing bespoke role-plays you can be left to facilitate the session on your own. Increasingly these days this might be done for reasons of economy, and the role-play company should have let you know that you will be running the session on your own. Let's assume this is the case.

You have been given a group of three people and have made your way to a breakout room with a certain amount of time to take them through their scenarios. First of all you should divide up the time appropriately. For example, if you are being given a ninety-minute slot and three people, it might seem obvious that each person will get thirty minutes. Setting up the session and explaining how you wish to proceed is probably going to take ten minutes at the beginning. Divide the remaining time between the three students and make a mental note as to when you should be finishing each role-play. Time management is an incredibly important part of these sessions. There will be other actors doing sessions simultaneously with yours, and you will all be expected back in the main seminar room at the same time with the feedback from your various sessions. If you overrun by ten minutes, the rest of the group in the main room will end up waiting for you.

Confidentiality

Explain to the participants how the bespoke session will work. That they will each work with you on a scenario that they want to role-play and that you will be whoever they want you to be. You should emphasise at this point that they don't have to use the real name of the person in the scenario, but that everything in the session will be entirely confidential so, if they want to, they can be comfortable with using real names. Often when they describe the situation the other people in the room will know the person the participant is talking about, particularly if they all work for the same company.

How to Run the Session

Work out an order of play. I often start by saying something like 'Now the most difficult question of the afternoon is who's going to go first?' Not the most hilarious or original of openers, I know, but it usually breaks the ice, provokes a laugh and gets a volunteer, and as they say 'a volunteer is worth a thousand pressed men'. It also may be useful at the end of the role-play when you can add into the feedback 'and of course you were absolutely brilliant by going first'.

Once the group have committed to a running order, turn to the first person and start taking the brief.

Who do you want me to be?

Ultimately, by the end of the brief you need to have enough information to create the person you are going to play and know the setting in which the role-play will take place. I always think about the information given on the page at the beginning of those wonderful old acting editions published by Samuel French.

- List of characters.

- Time and place.

At this point, then, as you face the participant for the first time you can ask one of two questions.

- What is the situation?

Or:

- Who do you want me to be?

You will need to ask both these questions, but the order in which you ask them can be quite important.

If you ask the situation question first, the participant can give you an awful lot of information about the situation, which it might be difficult for you to understand. Remember: no matter how much you know about the company you're working with, you will not understand all their practices and their behaviours. If someone starts to talk to you about a meeting that requires knowledge of an in-house reporting system that you do not have, the situation may not make immediate sense to you, and you will have to ask a lot more questions.

Ideally, taking a brief for a bespoke role-play should take no longer than five minutes and should involve as few questions as possible.

If your first question is 'Who do you want me to be?' the participant will immediately start creating a character for you. Hopefully they will give you a name, or if they are in any way reticent about this they will at least give you a job title.

> 'I want you to be a member of my team who's in charge of scheduling.'

> 'I want you to be a senior partner who I have to report to.'

At this point you don't necessarily have to press them for a name. You will need a name in order to do the role-play, but as long as you have got an idea of who you are you can then progress on to the question:

> 'And what is our meeting about?'

Ask about 'the meeting' rather than 'the situation'. If you ask about the situation you may start to get the following sort of information:

> 'Well about three years ago Raymond came to work here and he's not very tidy and messes up his desk and I find it very distracting and then several times he's been late but one of the main things is that in the office he is much more popular than I am and I'm finding this rather difficult...'

...and so on.

None of this is information that you will find particularly useful for the face-to-face meeting you are about to undergo.

So make the question as specific as possible:

> '...and what is our meeting about?'

Hopefully now you will have focused their mind onto the sort of specifics you need. For example, from the above information, they may now tell you that they need to have a meeting with Raymond in order to address the fact that his desk is often a mess and people can't find things on it when they go to his section of the office.

By now you should have a grasp of the situation and who you are supposed to be.

But do you have anything that you can build a character on? Anything that you can play?

You know that Raymond has a messy desk but this doesn't really give you anything that you can play as an actor. You need to gain some information that can help you create a believable character. And we have to remember that this character has to be believable from the point of view of the person you're having a meeting with. It would be wrong of them to expect you to do an impersonation of Raymond, but it's your job as a role-player to get the feel of Raymond and the sort of person he is. This may well be at the root of the problem that the participant had (or is going to have) at the meeting about the messy desk.

You need a question to give you something that you can play.

Ask the participant to give you three words that they feel describe Raymond.

People can find this very hard indeed.

They may start off with a reply such as 'well Raymond can be a bit of a...'

Gently redirect them. You need adjectives or adverbs.

For example, if the participant were to give you the words 'forceful, evasive, loud', you'd have a great starting point for your portrayal of Raymond in the role-play.

Edge them slowly towards giving you these three single words. They may give you something such as 'doesn't listen'. I would gently point out that that's two words, but that it's very helpful.

They won't always give you negative words and you shouldn't encourage them to, but make sure they give words you can play. It may be just a personal thing but I find it very difficult to play someone who they say is 'empathetic'. Probably because I come from Yorkshire! I'd find it easier to play someone who they say is 'caring'.

This is also a great time to ask for some sample dialogue. You can say to the participant: 'What are the sort of things that Raymond might say?' They might give you a phrase – for example, here Raymond might say: 'Well, one man's mess is another man's organisation.'

You can guarantee that if you manage to get this phrase or a slight hybrid of it into the conversation you'll find that it gets positive feedback from the participant after the role-play is over. Sometimes it might feel as if you are crowbarring the phrase into the scene, but it nearly always guarantees your being told afterwards 'You were just like him!' It's a little like doing an accent as an actor. If you can pick up on four or five key words or sounds, the general lilt and timbre of your speech will sound convincing. You haven't got time to do a full analysis of the accent, but what you will achieve is a very passable sound.

Here you haven't got time to build a full character based on Raymond from an in-depth psychological analysis of him with the participant, but by getting two or three key qualities of their perception of Raymond, you will give a convincing portrayal.

What's the point?

The final thing you need in order to make the role-play successful is to ask the participant what they want to achieve. What does success look like for them? At the end of the meeting with Raymond, where would they like to be?

Probably the simplest question that you can ask is:

'What is your objective?'

Make sure that this is as definable as possible. As you do more and more role-play work you will come to understand lots of management speak. One of the things that you might use here are SMART objectives. These are objectives that are:

S   specific

M   measurable

A   attainable

R   relevant

T   timed

In a short, five-minute meeting, which is ultimately what you want this role-play to be, it may not be realistic to think that you can come up with an objective that fits all five criteria, but if you work towards this you can't go far wrong.

So they may respond to you by saying:

> 'I want Raymond to understand the importance of keeping his desk tidy and I want us to agree how he will do this and the fact that I will check on this for the next three weeks.'

How much of this you are actually going to let them achieve is up to how well you think they manage the conversation, but at least you have an idea of where they are aiming, and something to judge them by.

The more specific the objective, the easier it is to guide where the role-play is going. You might find it difficult if the participant says that their objective is for Raymond to understand better the importance of tidiness. Much easier if they can come up with an objective that is achievable in this meeting.

> 'I want a plan in place as to how Raymond will improve his tidiness.'

You are now almost ready to begin the role-play.

Just one final thing. You should ask where the meeting would take place. Is this supposed to be in the participant's office, in which case they should be sitting down and you will walk up to the table? Are they coming to see you in your workplace, in which case the reverse should happen?

Sometimes they might say: 'Oh, I just find a meeting room.' In which case you'd both sit down together. This is useful for you as it is good scene-setting. At this point you can stand up and let them place the seats where they would like them. The participant may not do anything, or they may choose to move the seats. All this is great for your feedback. Where you sat and how they managed the placing of the seats will be important. Having an interview across a desk can feel very different from two seats placed at the corner of the desk to create a place for a conversation. All useful points for how you felt during the meeting when you get to your feedback.

You either checked with a facilitator, or you know yourself from having worked out your timings for the session, how long you have got, so now is the time to start the role-play.

Exactly the same rules apply here as applied for the performance of the pre-briefed role-play.

One feature that the facilitator may want you to use doing bespoke role-plays is the time-out.

Taking time out

This is a technique you can use to help the participant maximise their learning during the role-play. It's a bit like 'live pause' on your Sky box, and that is often a good way to introduce it to the participants. You have to face the fact that many people you will work with hate the whole idea of role-play. This might manifest itself in a loud groan when the facilitator announces that there are actors here to work with the participants during the session. Many people will only have experienced role-play by having done it with their colleagues. The memory may not be a good one. Working with a professional actor such as you will be a totally new and different experience for them. You do need to sell it in, however. Get them on side.

Probably the worst way you could introduce yourself is to say:

> 'Hello. I'm an actor and I'm here to do some role-play with you'.

This is guaranteed to get people heading for the door. I tend to use something along the lines of:

> 'I'm an actor, working in communication skills and I'm here to help work through any issues that you'd like to look at.'

There's nothing you can really do if people are against role-play. I have had people who have flatly refused to do it. If there is a facilitator working with you then this is their responsibility. If you're working in a small group and you yourself are facilitating, then the best way to cope with this is to acknowledge their reluctance and to start the session with someone else. If the session goes well it's very rare that the reluctant participant will still refuse to take part by the end of it.

One of the participant's main worries is that they have to sit down and face you and run through the whole scenario they have outlined to the end while their colleagues watch them make a mess of it. To counter this you can inform them that they can take a time-out at any point during the role-play. They can simply say 'time-out' or you can show them the acknowledged symbol, which is making a 'T' sign with the index fingers of both hands.

A time-out stops the role-play where it is. The facilitator, whether it is you or someone else, should then ask why the participant has taken time out, and what they want help with. They may come up with something along the lines of: they don't know what to say next, and they want their colleagues to make a suggestion. Rather than leave them with the sense that they have stopped and failed, you can at this point just introduce the beginning of the feedback session.

'Okay. Before we get suggestions from the group as to what to say, tell me about what you've done so far that you're happy with?'

This allows an atmosphere of positive feedback to come into the room. (You will learn more about how to phrase the positive feedback in the next chapter.)

After the time-out, you can allow the participant to choose the suggestion they want to take forward. Wind the action back a little to something you said, and use that line to cue them in. Just as at the beginning of the role-play, you should take the initiative to restart the proceedings.

It's a good idea to check with the facilitator, if you're working with one, that they're happy with the idea of using the time-out, but it really can take the pressure off for the participant. It means that the learning can actually be incorporated into the role-play as it progresses.

On many courses there is no longer time for every participant to do their role-play, receive feedback, and rerun the role-play. So the time-out can help learning be put into practice immediately.

The time-out can be used in any form of role-play, but it is particularly effective in bespoke role-play when you're dealing with a scenario that the participant has created themselves. You will also find yourself using it if you are playing the role of the actor/facilitator in a Forum Theatre, of which more later.

Summary

- Remember, it's for them and not for you.

- Make sure you understand the objective for the participant.

- Make sure that you have fully prepared the brief if there is one.

- Ask who you are, what the situation is and for three character words to play, if it's a bespoke role-play.

- Keep the performance level real.

- Don't push things to a climax.

- Beware of dumping all the information from your brief straight away. Let the participant work and earn the information as you progress.

- Do provide a level of challenge appropriate to each participant.

- Monitor what they are saying and doing so that you can use it for your feedback later.

Taking the brief

There are occasions when you sit down opposite a participant and start to investigate a bespoke brief and you uncover communication issues that you might never have dreamt of.

One such instance happened to me a couple of years ago in Sheffield. I was doing a role-play job for a major health-care provider which has a huge number of call handlers, people who handle patient enquiries on the telephone. The person I was to role-play with was a jocund, middle-aged lady from South Yorkshire.

'I don't do role-play,' she said, in a voice that would have easily carried to the back of the Open Air Theatre, Regent's Park, 'But I do have an issue.'

'Okay. Tell me about it.' I said.

'Well, I've got a member of my team who's just started on the telephone,' she boomed, 'and he's not particularly good at understanding people. I think he learnt all the test phone calls in the training by heart, which is how he passed, but now he's actually on the telephone talking to people we've had a couple of problems. I had a meeting with him last week and it didn't go too well. It might be quite nice to have a look at that.'

'What was the meeting about?'

'It was really about the fact that his English is not very good. He doesn't speak it very well and I think he understands it even less.'

I sensed that this might be the moment to move her into doing a role-play, so I suggested that I sit down opposite and we start. In reality, the staff member she had been dealing with had been Indian by the name of Rajit. I explained to her that my Indian accent tended to slip towards Cardiff all too quickly, and perhaps I could do an Eastern European accent in which I'm slightly more proficient.

'Okay then,' she replied, 'you can be an Eastern European called Rajit!'

I sat down opposite her and we began. She was not lost for words. Any hesitancy about role-play seemed to vanish in an instant as she launched into the meeting.

'Now, Rajit, I do have a few problems with how you're dealing with people on the telephone. I don't think you really understand what they're saying a lot of time, do you, love?'

She did not wait for a reply.

'I mean yesterday, that lady who rang in the morning. The one you filled in the patient form for, it just wasn't right, was it? For one thing, are you absolutely sure her name was Vaginal Discharge?'

I'm glad to say that it has only happened once in my role-play career but I just could not help it. I laughed. I laughed and I laughed. I laughed until the tears ran down my cheeks. A fellow female role-player sitting in the room tried to bury her shaking shoulders in her folder, but to no avail.

The issue was absolutely genuine. The event had really occurred, and sadly as a result of the meeting poor Rajit had in reality been dismissed, but his legacy was pure comedy gold.

Just be aware that, as you take any bespoke role-play brief, you are delving into someone's real life. It can be tragic or it can be highly comic. Whatever it is, it will be the greater for being real.

Here is the answer card to the role-play brief exercise:

Name – Robin Stevenson.

Works in admin providing backup services for client. Glide-time working.

I tend to work 8 a.m. – 4 p.m. – very useful early mornings work for firm. (*PLUS POINT.*)

I need to finish at 4 p.m. for 'family reasons'. (*KEEP QUIET IF POSSIBLE.*)

If pushed in correct manner, reveal horse-feeding problems, childcare problems and family time important to me.

Prepared to listen to solutions that help me work flexible hours.

You don't really need much more information than this to make the role-play work.

5

Feedback…

And How to Give It

One dictionary definition of the word feedback is 'an unpleasant noise caused by transmitter and receiver being located too close together'.

Sometimes that is exactly what we get at the end of a role-play.

However, if we break the word down we get a different perspective:

Feed – to nourish.

Back – to support.

And in essence that's what we're trying to do when we give feedback at the end of the role-play. We are trying to nourish and support the person who's just gone through the scenario.

Imagine you're in a rehearsal and you have just run a scene. Possibly for the first time. You stop and together with your fellow actors you turn towards the director and await his comments. What are the first words you want to hear? 'Good, great, excellent, well done.' You want something to validate what you've just done. You don't want undeserved praise, but you do want them to acknowledge that you have just run the whole scene. You don't want the sort of comment a young actor I worked with once received. Having run a long and difficult scene as Prince Florizel in Act Four of Shakespeare's *The Winter's Tale*, the director turned to him and said: 'Adequate.' Damned with faint praise – I don't think he ever really recovered.

Giving feedback is probably the most important skill for a good role-player. I don't think I've ever known a role-player who's not been re-employed simply because of the performances given, and believe me I've seen some pretty dodgy ones. If Equity cards were driving licences then I've been in sessions where quite a few penalty points should have been handed out. On the other hand, I have known actors who have not been re-employed because the facilitator or the person organising the course felt that their feedback skills were weak. An excellent female role-player, who I worked with on many occasions and who I thought was rather good, did a job with me for a banking client in the City of London. I don't know whether she was just having an off-day or what, but after two role-plays she sat round with the participants and her feedback was rather unspecific and a little fluffy. The consultant who was running the course just said to me at the end of the day: 'I don't think we'll use her again', and true to his word he's never asked to book her again since that incident back in 2007.

So as your starting point, think how you yourself would like to receive notes.

The first and most important thing to acknowledge is that, as soon as the role-play has ended – whether the feedback is led by the facilitator or yourself – the focus of attention should be on the participant. Remember they are not used to doing this. Some of them may have found it difficult. Some of them may have even found it traumatic, and some of them, almost certainly, won't have been very good at it. They'll want to say this almost immediately, so the importance of managing the correct order of feedback is paramount.

The order of feedback should really always be as follows:

1. Positive feedback from the participant themselves.

2. Positive feedback from yourself.

3. Positive feedback from the group.

4. Developmental feedback from the participant.

5. Developmental feedback from you.

6. Developmental feedback from the rest of the group.

If you are working in a group with a facilitator, check at the very beginning of the session how they would like the feedback to run. Obviously their word is law, but if you can begin to understand the following process, you will have an order of feedback that will help the participant get the most out of the role-play and help you make sure your comments are correctly placed, supportive and valued.

1. Positive Feedback from the Participant

So, immediately after the role-play the first question that should be asked of the participant is:

> 'What do you feel you did well?'

In most instances they will start to say that they didn't do anything well at all and they made a terrible mess of it. This may well be true. You cannot let the first feedback they give be negative. Your job is to guide them towards generating some positive comments.

Think of your own experience at the end of a performance. It's almost guaranteed that the things that will stay in your mind are the things that you're not happy with, rather than the successes of the evening. Self-deprecation seems to be part of human nature, but it's something that we should not encourage in the immediate aftermath of a role-play.

After a little thought they will begin to come up with some positive points. You don't necessarily need to acknowledge them, although if you agree with the participant you might do, but make sure that the participant has a chance to say whatever they need to say at this point.

[69]

2. Positive Feedback from You

The second person to speak in the order of feedback should be you. With *your* positive comments. It's important that your positive comments are personal. After all, they are your opinion, and they are coming from you, the person who experienced the role-play with the participant.

Fergus McLarnon, now director of Role-plays for Training, says that on his first role-play the best piece of advice he was offered was 'just remember three things that they said to you'. It is a piece of advice that has never left him, and although he's now been doing role-play for many years, it's still his starting point for feedback with any participant.

But how do you give that feedback? How do you frame it so as not to provoke the response which one role-player reported – 'How dare you come in here with your pathetic play-acting?'

You should really base it on the principle of 'say what you see'.

Phrases such as 'I liked' are very good. No one can argue with that. If you say 'It was good…', then a facilitator or a consultant working alongside you might have cause to disagree if you have commented on something they feel the participant shouldn't have done.

The advantage of allowing the participants to give their feedback first and encouraging them to be positive is that it also gives you time to start getting your feedback together. You have to have something to say of a very positive nature as soon as a facilitator asks you or as soon as it's your turn to give feedback.

Go back to the rehearsal situation. The scene ends and you look at the director. That look is saying: 'Well, what did you think? How did I do?' The longer the pause before his reply, the less convinced you are by his eventual: 'Yeah, that was good.'

So you need to have your feedback ready to go. Some people find it difficult to immediately process feedback having been involved in the role-play.

I always liken this to the process going on in your mind when you are acting. Although you believe you are in character all the time, living your character's feelings, and experiencing your character's emotions, a tiny bit of your brain disengages from all that and looks after what is expected of you as an actor. It's what makes you stand in the right light, move and exit out of the right door and do the blocking as directed.

In a role-play, therefore, although at the time you're fully engaged in character in the role-play with the participant, that portion of your brain can be engaged in checking how they are doing. These are the things you can then say as soon as you need to give feedback. I'll list them all in full later, and some are easier to remember than others. In a way it's a clever mix of the Stanislavskian and the Brechtian both working together.

The point here is that the first thing the participant should hear is some positive language. However, you don't want to just pour unspecific praise onto them. If this happens, human nature tends to decree that we ignore it and want people to start finding fault and become more critical of what we're doing. It is essential that we validate the positive feedback and to do this we can use a process called 'instancing'.

Instancing

Here I am extremely grateful to the actress Francesca Ryan, with whom I've had the pleasure and privilege of doing more role-plays than I can remember!

We often teach role-play technique together, and she explains the joys of instancing really well.

[71]

'That was great.'

'I felt you did that really well.'

'I liked how positive you made me feel.'

'You made me feel annoyed.'

'You just sort of irritated me.'

'You didn't listen much, I didn't really feel you understood.'

It's all too easy to find yourself using these kinds of generalities in giving feedback. Unfortunately, they aren't much use to a participant.

Feedback needs to be specific.

What did a participant do well? Or *what* could they have done differently? Give them an *instance*.

'It was really helpful when you offered to go through the timetable with me.'

'I felt irritated when you interrupted twice during my answer about last year's figures.'

In order to give specific instances, you need to be gathering evidence as the role-play progresses. One part of your brain needs to be remembering what the participant says and does during the role-play, as well as playing your role. Otherwise, when it comes to giving feedback, you are simply giving your subjective opinion on how they did. A participant can take or leave what you say, unless you have instances to back it up.

Using instances, you can give feedback on what you felt during a role-play.

Avoid using the phrase 'you made me feel…'

The participant hasn't 'made' you feel anything. If the feeling you had wasn't positive, using 'you made me feel' could come across as judgemental. Or even accusatory. We instinctively resist feedback that places the emotional burden on us. 'You made me feel' invites the unspoken response: 'No, I didn't!'

What you feel belongs to you. Own your own feeling. Leave the participant to draw their own conclusions from your observation. The following is a useful formula. Particularly if the feedback about your feelings might be uncomfortable for the participant.

> 'When you made eye contact with me, I felt that I was being listened to.'

It uses specific instances to communicate how you felt:

> 'When you praised my work on the January project, I felt really valued.'

> 'When you were drumming your fingers on the desk, I felt irritated.'

Taking it one step further, you might invite a participant to reflect for themselves on what they said or did:

> 'When you said I was obviously not coping, I felt confused. I'm wondering if there's another way of putting that?'

> 'When you started telling me which model I should buy without asking me any questions, I felt myself switching off. I'm wondering why you chose to do it that way?'

This is powerful because it leaves the participant in the driving seat.

Note that you are not telling the participant what to say or how to say it. That's not your job.

There's no point in overloading the positive feedback. I would suggest that two or, at the very most, three points are what you need.

If you cannot come up with real positive feedback backed up by evidence from what the participant has done during the role-play, then a couple of easy feedback openers are:

'Well done. You got through it and no matter what
happens it won't be as hard in the real world now.'

If you repeat that verbatim I'm sure it will sound a little hollow, but if you change it into your own words, it can be a good opener when you're really grasping for things to say.

If things have gone really badly then there is always:

'You have a really well-modulated vocal tone!'

I have no idea what it means, but then hopefully neither will they. If it's delivered with a smile it should do the trick and allow you to move on to the next part of the feedback process.

3. Positive Feedback from the Group

This is allowing the group to come up with their positive comments.

You should be careful here. If the participant has had trouble bringing up something positive, and you have had trouble bringing up something positive, then you can guarantee that the group will not be overflowing with praise. If members of the group start making comments such as: 'Your eye contact was good, but I felt that...' close them down immediately. Point out that at this stage you only want to focus on the positive comments. If you feel things are a little ropey it might be as well to move straight on to section 4 and ask the participant what they feel they might have done differently.

4. Developmental Feedback from the Participant

Rather than categorising the feedback as good and bad, or positive and negative, most training professionals refer to positive feedback and *developmental* or *constructive* feedback. It does not take a PhD in communication skills to see that these are both euphemisms for 'negative'! It is useful, however, to think of all feedback as positive, so the use of these words can help. When managing feedback, you should speak in non-comparative terms. It's important that you and the participant do not start saying things are good or bad, better or worse, effective or less effective. The question you should probably ask them is:

'What do you feel you might have done differently?'

This will allow them to mention several things that they feel unhappy with. Sometimes the participant can bring up things in this section that you feel they actually did quite well and it's fine to say: 'Well, I felt that that was very good', as long as you can link it with some actual evidence, i.e. by instancing. In the main, though, they will come up with points that you will probably agree could have been dealt with differently. If, for example, they say: 'I could have looked more interested,' you could ask them how they feel that might have been achieved.

It's always much more effective to get them to propose a solution rather than you. Remember you are not in the session to be a solution provider. You are there to shine a torch on the behaviour shown by the participants and to help them determine what would work better. If they work it out for themselves, they will remember it more.

5. Developmental Feedback from You

If there are any golden rules, then one is probably that you shouldn't give more 'developmental' feedback than you have given positive feedback. To tell them they have a well modulated vocal tone and a firm handshake, and then to give them fourteen points which they might like to think about doing differently, is probably not a good balance.

There is a school of thought espoused by some childcare books that you should give twelve pieces of positive feedback for each piece of developmental feedback. Personally I don't know how the child ever gets time to do anything, but I agree that the balance should aim to fall on the side of the positive.

You can also add weight to your developmental feedback by the use, once again, of instancing.

For example:

> 'When you looked up from the papers and made eye contact, I felt very much part of the conversation.'

That says that what they did that helped you to feel better.

As with all developmental feedback, how it is phrased is incredibly important. As you saw earlier in the process of instancing, you need to be very aware of the phrase: 'It made me…' As in: 'When you said I'd been late for several days, you made me feel very angry.' This is very important. They didn't actually make you do anything. That was how you felt as a result of what they said, and that should be made clear when you give feedback. A better way of phrasing that might be:

> 'When you said I'd been late for several days, I felt very angry.'

This keeps your feeling separate from their actions. Hopefully it will allow them to draw the conclusion that if they had taken a different action, you would have felt differently.

This is your purpose in a role-play. By allowing the participant to act out the situation and allowing them to know how you felt, it can help them arrive at choosing different behaviours that they might use in the situation.

Some good topics of feedback that are easy to spot are as follows:

Eye contact

When people look us in the eye we feel as though they have nothing to hide. People who conduct meetings looking down at papers on the table, or letting their eyes wander round the room, do not inspire trust in us. If that is what the participant is trying to do, i.e. deliver an open and honest message that they believe in, make sure that the eye contact they are giving you matches the message. Lack of it can make them appear shifty and untrustworthy. Not good in so many professions.

Open questions

An open question is a question that cannot be answered by the words 'yes' or 'no'. Words that begin open questions are 'How', 'What' and 'Why'. Of these, 'How' is undoubtedly the best.

Imagine someone sitting down in a meeting and asking you: 'Did you have a good journey?' You could answer with a straightforward 'yes' or 'no' and they really would be none the wiser about your situation. But if they used the question: 'How was your journey?' you would have to give them more information. The two bonus points here are that they have more information to work with, and this can help them ask other questions and hear more about what you want. The second benefit is that people always feel good while they're talking about things connected with themselves. This means that the person doing the talking may start coming up with answers and will certainly leave the meeting feeling better. So keep on the lookout for open questions.

So if 'How' is the best open question, then a close second is 'What', as in: 'What was your journey like?' This might tend to produce a more factual response, whereas 'How' may have allowed the person to answer with some emotional content.

'Why' is good but can be a little interrogative and should be used with care.

'Where', of course, is technically a closed question, as in 'Where do you come from?' allowing the one-word answer – 'Rotherham' – and then no doubt a deep-scarlet blush if they really do come from Rotherham! 'Where' can be useful in the context of the summary of a meeting. After a discussion, the participant may ask you: 'Right now, so where are we?' and this is a good way of getting you to summarise what has happened in the meeting.

One thing that people sometimes do is close down an open question. They may ask 'How was your journey?', and pause for a second. If they don't receive an immediate answer, they'll tend to follow up with 'Was it okay?' Which of course is a closed question and you can then answer with 'yes' or 'no'.

Other questions

There are two other modes of questioning that you can listen for, and, of course, use yourself.

Sometimes you can't come up with an open question when one is needed, and yet it would be useful to get more information from the person rather than just move on to the next question. For example, you may have asked a nice open question such as: 'How was your journey here this morning?' only to get the reply: 'Okay.'

You need more information, but you don't want to shut things down with a closed question such as: 'Was it difficult?' So you might think about using the expression: 'Tell me more.'

In the example above a participant may say:

> 'How have you been coping with your workload lately?'
>
> 'Okay.'
>
> 'Oh really. Tell me more.'

This shows that the participant understands the value of questioning and exploring, and this is the behaviour you might wish to comment on and reward. As in all positive behaviours, you should make the phrase your own, but, whatever you say, the principle of exploring and digging down into an answer remains true.

Reflecting

Very similar to this is the technique of reflecting. Here, rather than follow their answer with a question on a new topic, you reflect back the word that the person has just said to stimulate another response.

For example:

> 'I'm rather worried about this transaction.'
>
> 'Worried?'
>
> 'Yes, it's all rather new ground and strange territory, and I'm looking for someone to help out.'

Both of the above techniques are immensely useful to you as a role-player in getting the participant to do more talking when you require it. Reflecting back their own language should get them talking, and asking them to expound on an answer will always produce more information.

So, as well as being good techniques that you can give positive feedback on when used by a participant, these are also useful tools for you as a role-player.

Use of silence

This also applies to questions. Having asked a good question, it can sometimes take a person a few seconds or so to come up with a good answer. In fact, you the role-player might need a short pause in order to come up with the answer that you know they want to hear. Don't be afraid to take it. If they are not comfortable with silence, they will probably break the pause, either with a rephrasing of the question, or a secondary question. Both of which will probably be easier to answer and gain them less information. When you have asked the question, wait for the answer.

Listening skills

As I said earlier with reference to the great Sir Ralph Richardson, listening is an extremely important part of acting. It is also an incredibly important part of communication skills in general, and hopefully it is something that a participant will display in the role-play. It's certainly something you can comment on in your feedback.

Evidence of good listening skills probably starts with good eye contact.

> 'I noticed you were looking at me throughout the conversation, and I really felt as though you were listening to me.'

The speaker needs to demonstrate active listening skills here. They can use small noises such as 'um' or 'ah' or 'okay' to ensure that the dialogue is maintained, but a good listener will do more than this.

When you say something as the character you are playing in the role-play, the participant can sometimes respond to you by summarising what you have said to show that they've been listening. For example, they may begin with: 'So you're saying that…' And then restate the last thing you said. If they use the exact words that you used (not saying 'scared' instead of 'afraid', for instance), you can compliment them on 'using exactly the same words'. To quote the well-known phrase: 'We're speaking the same language.' This brings both people closer together.

When you feel that the participant is actively listening to you, it will help you feel much more confident that they are really communicating the message to you. It can also help you feel more positive about yourself and the message they're communicating.

Most of the above will come as common sense to you as an actor after having taken part in the scenario. As an actor, you're very capable of analysing behaviour and why people do certain things in certain situations. Your training as an actor has helped you think about why one line is said as the result of another. It is what helps you to create a character and work your way through a scene in a rehearsal room. This is the process we are using in the role-play with the exception that the scene is unrehearsed, and one person involved isn't an actor.

Remember you are not there to be a solution provider. You are there to help the participant see the issue for what it is by playing it out in a safe environment. It's very easy to get caught up in saying what you feel people should do rather than letting them work out their own solutions.

Go back once more to the rehearsal room and think of how you work best with a director. Are you at your best when told absolutely what to do? How do you feel when a director, or heaven forefend, another actor, says, 'What you should do here is…?' Perhaps you begin to feel limited in your creativity, and start thinking of what is right or wrong. Perhaps you immediately decide that you want to do something very different from their suggestion.

As a young actor, I once worked for a director who gave me every move right down to the gestures. This left me going on stage each evening thinking that the performance was all about getting it right rather than making any creative contribution of my own. I'm pretty sure that my work as a result was rather dreadful. Stilted, unoriginal and trying to reproduce what I'd been told to do rather than doing the things I felt I could do.

The clever director gets you to do what he wants but makes you think that it's your idea. This is exactly what your feedback should help the participant to do. For example, in the role-play, you may have noticed that the participant spoke very quickly with hardly any pauses so that you found it very difficult to take on board all the information that was given to you. So you give them feedback: 'I found it rather difficult to take everything in.' And you instance this by saying: 'An awful lot of information was given in a very short space of time, and there was no time for me to stop and think about anything that was said.'

The participant may well be nodding and accepting this feedback, but that doesn't necessarily mean that they know how to improve. You know full well as the recipient of the information that if there had been more pauses it would have been easier to take it all in. You can easily just say to the participant: 'I think you should pause more.'

This may well produce the result that you want. However, to be comfortable with a pause, a person has to be comfortable with silence. You have just told them that they need to pause, but they may not necessarily have understood exactly why. And if you then go on and replay a portion of the role-play the participant may be adding in pauses without understanding the reason behind it. To an extent, here, you have provided a solution, and as I have said several times, a role-player is not a solution provider.

What you could do is to open them up to the possibilities that there were other behaviours they might have used in that situation. You can often use the phrase 'I wonder' to start the participant thinking about a change in behaviour. For example, here one might say: 'I wonder what it might be like if there were more pauses.'

You have made a suggestion as to the solution here, but you have not told the participant exactly what to do. Just the same as if a director might say to you: 'I wonder what it might be like if you were to come through the door more quickly.' In such a case, all but the most obstructive actors would be keen to give it a try. If it works and feels good, then you'll be keen to use it and it won't be too long before you think that the idea of the very quick entrance was your own. The director doesn't mind. You're happy, and his name is still on the poster!

Here the participant will think about what the effect of more pauses might be. If you're replaying the role-play, then they'll have the chance to put it into practice. If you're not, then at least it might open up a discussion as to the value of the pause in any conversation, and they can go away thinking that it's a good idea and one that they themselves came up with.

All the above are just some of the things you might wish to draw on to give as feedback after a role-play.

The Feedback Sandwich

Sometimes the feedback isn't portioned out between the participant, yourself and the group. The facilitator controlling the group may decide to come to you and ask for your feedback first. Always try and turn this straight back to the participant. A quick 'Well done' never goes amiss, followed by '…And what do you feel you did well there?'

The facilitator may have already done this and may turn to you and say. 'Okay, what feedback do you have?'

Essentially you are going to stick to the pattern I have already laid out, but you're going to have to use all the feedback together in one opportunity and create what is known as 'The Feedback Sandwich.' This is three pieces of feedback given together. It acts as a guide as to how you might give your feedback. Some trainers think that this is a little formulaic, and indeed if it's stuck to too rigidly, then it will become inauthentic. Some trainers know it as 'The Shit Sandwich'. The reason will become apparent.

The bread is the positive feedback. The filling of the sandwich is the developmental feedback.

So you may just have done a role-play with a sales-team manager who has told you that you need to increase your figures. They've done reasonably well in the role-play, and the facilitator has already asked them what they thought of it. They thought they were good. This is not unheard of.

You may now be squirming inside because you know the opposite to be true. Believe me, this can happen. Use what they have said as a guide as to how to place your own feedback.

Your feedback sandwich may go something like this:

> 'I really liked the way that you stood up when I came
> into the meeting. I felt important when you did that
> and I felt that the meeting was worth taking notice of.
> I found it a little difficult to follow what you were
> saying when you had your head down in the papers
> on your desk to look for quotes and figures. I really
> liked the way you summarised the meeting at the end
> as I left knowing what was expected of me.'

So you have given two pieces of very positive feedback there. The greeting and the close of the meeting. You have drawn attention to the fact that this participant probably spent most of the rest of the meeting with his head buried in papers. However, you have not said that this was necessarily wrong, but you have referred to the effect it had on you during the meeting. The important thing is that you finished with something positive. This is what any feedback session should do.

Think back to that rehearsal and the notes from the director. No matter how many notes you have had that you feel you need to work on, you really want to end on 'Well done. I think there are lots of good things happening there, and you're on course for the opening night.'

Although the feedback sandwich may be a tried-and-tested formula, try and make it your own. Think about how you might give your three statements.

One good rule of thumb is to make sure they are not linked by the word 'but'. For example: 'I like the way you listened to me which I could see from your eye contact, but I felt that some of what I said was ignored.' The word 'but' has the effect of negating the first part of the feedback and rendering it worth less, or even worthless.

Think back to the director giving you notes:

'You were excellent in the first act but after the interval it all went down the drain!' The highs of the first act are now worth nothing.

If the praise is unconditional and unlinked it is stronger. 'You were fabulous in the first act. I thought that the second act went down hill somewhat.' It still says the same, but it allows each piece of feedback to breathe on its own.

You might say:

> 'I liked the way you listened to me, which I could see from the eye contact you gave me. I did feel that sometimes what I said was ignored as you didn't seem to summarise what I said.'

Each statement works on its own.

You can also use this technique as part of your own feedback to the participant. They may use the 'but' word in their role-play with you: 'You're a great worker, but you do turn up late.'

The 'great worker' statement now counts for nothing as all you have heard is the section after the 'but', which involves your lateness. You may feed back to them that it would have been more effective if their statements had been separate.

> 'You are a really good worker. There are several occasions on which you have been late.'

A little bald perhaps, but it does mean that the 'good worker' praise is not wasted. If this had been properly fleshed out, both these statements would work as good feedback to you in role.

So, if possible, keep the various components of your feedback sandwich separate.

In-role Feedback

One of the advantages of using a professional actor for role-play, rather than the company using their own people is that professional actors are capable of giving what is referred to as 'in-role feedback'

You give feedback to the participant from the character's point of view rather than stepping out of role and giving the feedback as yourself.

As actors in the rehearsal room, you will have had no problem discussing your character with a director or a fellow actor from the character's point of view. As in:

> 'I didn't feel that I'd stand up and move here. I just feel too shell-shocked.'

Or:

> 'I felt very angry as I said all that and looking at you made me feel rather helpless.'

All this helps you understand the character you're playing.

As feedback this can be incredibly effective. To a certain extent it allows you to break some of the rules I have just established for giving good, clear feedback. You are speaking from the point of view of how you felt as the character when the participant spoke to you, and in reality no one can question that.

This is where you will really come into your own in role-play. After they have played a scene, actors are used to expressing how they felt at any particular moment. On the other hand, for instance, when a doctor tells a patient the dreadful news that they have cancer, the doctor often has no idea how effective he or she is being as the person receiving the news cannot be asked how they're feeling, or what they feel about the doctor.

Yet in role-play this is possible.

You can feed back immediately after a role-play. The feedback doesn't have to be positive, but it should just be an honest assessment of how you felt playing the person receiving the news.

> 'I think I knew it was cancer, but when the doctor
> actually said the word it just felt terrible.'

The point of this sort of feedback is to enable the doctor to have an insight into both sides of the conversation. Not something they're going to get in real life, and therefore a real bonus that you can offer as an actor.

You should always establish with the facilitator beforehand what sort of feedback is required. Quite often in medical scenarios, such as the breaking of bad news, for example, the facilitator will want you to remain in character. They should still observe the order of feedback and make sure that they go to the doctor or participant first and check how he or she is feeling.

Then they will come to you.

> 'So how are you feeling, Mr Smith?'

Again, use the part of your brain that you use as an actor on stage to monitor what you're doing. The doctor has been through a difficult situation, so even if you as Mr Smith feel appalling, make sure you can put a positive slant on that so that the doctor can take something away from it.

> 'I think I knew it was cancer, but when the doctor
> actually said it I felt terrible. I was glad he'd said it

though. It sort of cleared the air, and although I feel terrible at least I now do know where I stand.'

There is no way that a doctor could expect you to feel good if you've just been told such terrible news, but at least it is an opportunity to acknowledge the fact that he or she has done some good straight-talking and clear messaging.

Your feedback skills will increase the more role-play you do. The more sessions you sit in on, the more examples of feedback from participants you will hear that you think are useful. You will gain valuable information from the good facilitators you work with, and a guide as to what not to say from the ones who aren't quite so effective.

The main rule as always, and indeed as in the role-play itself, is that less is more.

Remember you're not there as a solution provider. This can't be emphasised enough. Quite often one of the main failings of inexperienced role-players is that they feel they have to solve the problem the participant has brought to them, rather than just lead them through the playing out of the problem and help them to find a solution through this.

Summary

- The aim of feedback is to help and support the participant.

- The first piece of feedback should always be positive.

- Always backup feedback wherever possible with an instance of behaviour.

- Talk in terms of 'different', rather than in terms of 'good and bad'.

- Remember the feedback sandwich. This can shape your feedback, but doesn't have to be stuck to.

- You are expected to be able to give feedback as a role-player, but less is more if you don't have anything to say.

- Keep the positive feedback clear from the more developmental feedback. No 'buts' linking sentences.

- You don't have to have the answers.

- You have a great gift as an actor in that you can tell people how you felt when things happen. That should be the basis of any feedback that you give.

" The work I do as a corporate actor and facilitator never ceases to surprise and challenge me. I've had some amazing experiences, met some extraordinary people and visited some amazing places. It's in Moscow that two particularly memorable experiences occurred.

One was during the course of a session with two participants, when I sprang up to the flip chart to support a point I was making around use of flips in presentations and the inclusiveness and 'openness' of the presenter out front. As I reached for the marker pen I fumbled and dropped it in front of me, but continuing unfazed, like the pro I am, I reached down to pick it up only for the entire crotch seam of my suit trousers to tear. Remarkably this was undetected by the participants and I was faced with the choice of carrying on with carefully choreographed movement back to my seat or 'out' it! I went with the latter, and in a culture of privacy and formality, my disclosure about the whole experience, my inner monologue and the dilemma, was a total revelation to the female participant and consolidated my learning objective with greater clarity than a thirty-minute session could ever have done. I've considered using it in the future but though the work can be well paid, it can't support a new suit per job.

Later that evening, midnight saw the clock tip over to my thirty-third birthday. After dinner with colleagues earlier, a combination of tiredness and tensions saw them all retire early to bed leaving me to toast myself alone in the hotel bar. Or so I thought. The perk of this job is often the quality of hotels you experience, though there are caveats. I was quickly propositioned by not one but three 'ladies of the night'. I declined this particular 'role-play' job and retired to my room, alone, to turn on the breaking news of Michael Jackson's death.

A memorable day.

Robert Shaw Cameron

6

Forum Theatre...
And How to Do It

The third, and indeed increasingly popular, form of role-play that you should understand and be able to work with is Forum Theatre.

Forum Theatre, or 'Forum' as it is often referred to, has become much used in recent years as a training method, since it uses two actors who can work with a very large group.

Whereas bespoke role-play or pre-briefed role-play needs a ratio of one actor to a group of five or possibly six people for half a day, a Forum Theatre session can last one hour and two actors can successfully work in front of an audience of up to eighty or one hundred people. This, of course, makes Forum Theatre attractively financially viable for large organisations and public-sector bodies.

Forum Theatre, as used in the training world, is based on a theatre form brought into practice by the Brazilian theatre director Augusto Boal. He used the exercise as part of what he called his 'theatre of the oppressed'. During the process, audience members, or even the actors, could stop a scene in which one character was being oppressed in some way. The audience were allowed to suggest different actions for the actors to carry out onstage in an attempt to change the outcome of what they were seeing. Breaking down the barrier between actor and audience allowed the spectators to have a creative input into the dramatic action they were watching. Boal saw the audience as both actors and spectators, giving everybody a role in the process.

You will find that Forum is an incredibly popular form of role-play. Some large organisations have to train huge numbers of people. For example, local authorities are obliged to put their employees through diversity training, and this alone can involve several hundred people.

Diversity training is used to help increase cultural awareness, knowledge and skills on a range of subjects, such as disability, gender and sexuality. The assumption is that the training will benefit the organisation, promote better teamwork, and create a more inclusive workplace. Organisations will have a diversity policy in place, and the communication of this policy to their employees often uses Forum Theatre.

You will also find Forum being used on performance coaching. When, for example, Channel 4 changed its appraisal policy, all its employees had to be trained in the new appraisal process. A Forum Theatre session would be set up where a manager would conduct an appraisal with one of his team. Both the manager and the team member were played by actors in front of a group of about six or seven actual managers who together would work out the course the interview should take.

Sometimes Forum Theatre can be scripted but the action will stop at a particularly controversial point where the audience are asked how things should proceed. Many Forums, however, are fully improvised by both actors with nothing having been set in stone before the session begins.

As with all basic methodology, role-play companies will all have a slightly different version of Forum Theatre. You will come across facilitators and trainers who have made their own alterations to it.

Let's take a look at how a basic Forum Theatre might work, and then we can look at the changes that have been added to this process.

Forum Theatre: the Basics

Forum Theatre usually consists of two actors. One will work as an actor/facilitator. In this role you are the person who directly communicates with the audience. You manage their questions, their ideas and their opinions. You are the person who controls the Forum and decides how it moves forward.

The second actor will normally play the person with the problem or issue. For example, as the second actor in a Forum for teaching appraisal technique, you will play the person being appraised. In a diversity session for the local authority, perhaps, you would play the person who has the diversity issue. On a more practical level, the second actor is also a good person to help manage the time, making sure the session doesn't overrun.

As the second actor, you do not relate directly to the audience. You remain in character throughout, and although at some moments the audience may be able to ask how you felt when a particular thing was said, you are not in charge of the scene.

To differentiate these two roles I tend to call the first actor the facilitator and the second actor the anchor. Some people have different names for these roles, but their functions are roughly the same. In some instances, the two actors will also work alongside an independent facilitator. I'll look at how this changes things later.

You will be sent a Forum Theatre brief from the role-play company you are working for. In some instances the initial brief may be scripted. Let's look at this scenario first.

Scripted Forum

You have received a three-page duologue as your Forum Theatre script.

Learn it. Learn it well.

You may well only meet the other actor you will be performing opposite at the time of the job and may have little or no time to rehearse.

Let's look at an example of a script that might be used to begin a Forum Theatre session.

This script was written by Brian Jordan, who in my opinion is one of the best corporate writers in the business today. Having started out as an actor himself, he appreciates that having a corporate script that can also work as something for actors to be able play well is a distinct advantage.

Not all Forum scripts are as much fun as this.

This script was commissioned by a large law firm to front a Forum Theatre session on networking skills for younger lawyers and junior associates. It's a good script for actors in that it is playable, fun and, hopefully, has touches of humour.

Getting Work is a Full-time Job

A male lawyer – let's call him MILES WRIGHT *– approaches the middle table.*

MILES. Would you believe it – I got there and I'd forgotten what everybody wanted – (*Points at people in the audience.*) so it was a white wine, a half of crème de menthe, Sex on the Beach, a shandy with not too much lager in it please as it gives me headaches and a Baileys and Pernod with a paper umbrella, sparkler and swizzle stick. The barman was no help – even though he could see me struggling… he just said 'Fancy that – a lawyer cocking up at the bar.'

I hate these seminar networking things – Clifford Fluke thinks I should come here and tout for work like a common… work-touter-type person. You know, they may as well give me a big sign on a stick which says 'Lawyer Sale This Way –Visit Me for Discounted Advisory Work, Cut-Price Insolvencies, Negotiations by Negotiation' – with an arrow pointing downwards. You never meet any – hold on, who's that over there…?

He sees and points at the other actor.

Don't look, don't look, don't look – even though I'm pointing and saying 'who's that over there?' – don't be stupid enough to look at her. That is Amelia Brockman – a Director at Vanilla Hedgefunds. I tell you what – they're involved in the Conglomerate Holdings' restructuring... I'll go and butter her up with my terrific networking skills and get a bit of work for the company. Just stand back and take notes, cos 'partner' here I come.

He walks over to AMELIA.

(*Under breath.*) Name and something memorable about myself.

He gets to AMELIA.

Hello, I'm Miles Wright.

AMELIA. Amelia Brockman.

They shake hands.

MILES. I work for Clifford Fluke and I er... I once shot a rabbit.

AMELIA (*confused*). Congratulations.

MILES (*confused by his own choice*). Thanks. That's obviously not the most interesting thing about me.

AMELIA. No, I'm sure you've shot all sorts of animals.

MILES. Yeah, good one. No, I've done all sorts of, er... you know... lots of... very many, many... So... Family... are your parents dead?

AMELIA. No, both very much alive.

MILES. Thank heavens. I hate these things – don't you?

AMELIA. Well, I wouldn't say 'hate', exactly –

MILES. You can meet some really boring people – present company accepted, of course.

AMELIA. Likewise.

Pause. Nothing happening – MILES *is very stuck.*

So, Miles, what do you do?

MILES. Oh, you know – this 'n' that… expertise in all sorts of areas. I'm a sort of jack of all trades and master of them all as well. Moratoriums, work-outs, standstills, override arrangements – you name it – if it's in the legal ball park I've jumped up and sniffed it. You know, if it requires a corporate legal mind I've run it up the flagpole, bunged it at the wall, taken it for a test drive and got into bed with it.

AMELIA. Well done.

MILES. Thanks. How about you?

AMELIA. I work in hedge funds.

MILES. Crikey – hold tight or you'll lose your shirt. Or blouse. I'm not sexist in the general blouson area. But – (*Intake of breath.*) edge-of-the-seat stuff.

AMELIA. It has its moments.

MILES. I bet. Who do you work for?

AMELIA. Vanilla Hedgefunds.

MILES. Right – you're currently involved with… (*Rolls his hand to generate her to finish sentence.*)

AMELIA. Conglomerate Holdings Group.

MILES. Yes – they're the ones. Tough job?

AMELIA. Well, it's been in the press so…

MILES. Really – I've seen nothing about it in the *Daily Star*.

AMELIA. Somehow they must've missed it. We have a stakeholding in Conglomerate and it's in a bit of –

MILES. In that case – Clifford Fluke are the lawyers for you. We're the market leaders in all types of that sort of thing. It must be true – it says it on our website.

AMELIA. Yes, we've got a few problems though.

MILES. We could iron those problems out no trouble. We're really good.

AMELIA. Yes, but our problems are very specific.

MILES. They always are, but we deal with them. Partly because we're a fantastic law firm and partly because you won't pay us if we don't.

AMELIA. Yes, but we're just a small hedge fund and although I'm sure we'd be happy to pay your exorbitant fees –

MILES. Worth every penny…

AMELIA. – we'd be a little unsure as to whether we'd receive as much attention as your bigger institutional clients.

MILES. Yes, of course you would. Yes. Yes. Definitely. We always pay attention to the amount of attention we always pay and in your case we'd make no exception.

AMELIA. But Conglomerate Holdings are really based in the States – I heard your whole department left in the US – so can you still service clients who require expertise over there?

MILES. Yes. We're a global company – one big happy family – apart from the French arm who are a bit *dans leur derrières*. But that's the French for you. Look, let me give you my card. (*Produces a card and hands it over.*)

AMELIA (*reading it*). Spearmint Rhino Membership Ca–

MILES. Sorry, wrong one. (*Takes it back.*) There we are. (*Gives another but snatches back.*) The phone number's not right – let me change it for you. (*Checks his pockets.*) Got a pen?

AMELIA. Yes.

MILES. Top-notch. May I?

AMELIA. Course. (*Hands over the pen.*)

MILES. There we go.

He puts the pen back in his pocket and gives her the card.

AMELIA. Thanks. Can I have the pen back?

MILES. Sorry. (*Gives her pen.*) A hangover from my kleptomaniac days – you know, when I hung out with Richard Madeley.

AMELIA. Those must've been happy times.

MILES. You bet. Look, we could do this job for you, no probs. I may even be able to have a word on price.

AMELIA. That would be good.

MILES. Don't think I'm trying to sell us to you. I mean, if God had meant for me to be a vulgar, tacky salesman I'd have been born American.

AMELIA. There is that.

MILES. Right then… er… sorry, what did you say your name was again?

AMELIA. Amelia.

MILES. Course, I knew that, I mean I said 'Amelia' to them over there when I was trying to avoid you – but it just slipped my mind.

AMELIA. Fine.

MILES. Right, well, I really must leave. Not leave you – you're not boring me or anything – it's just that it's time I left the entire function.

AMELIA. Well, I'd like to say it's been a pleasure.

MILES. No trouble. And I can't wait to get started on our business together.

AMELIA. No – I bet you can't.

MILES. Cheerio.

AMELIA. Bye.

> AMELIA *goes and* MILES *walks back to where he started – by the table.*

MILES (*as he walks*). Johnny Big Potatoes partner – here I come.

Many scripts that you receive will be much drier than this and much more factual.

First of all, read through the script and make sense of it. Then if you are the actor/facilitator, make sure you understand the learning points that are to be drawn out of it.

These will have been sent to you by the role-play company, or the client. If you haven't been sent them in advance then make sure you have time when you arrive for the session to speak to the client or the facilitator.

If you are the second actor, or anchor, you will also need to know and understand these learning points.

In the above script, the actor playing Miles would work as the actor/facilitator, inviting the audience to tell him what he did well and what he might change. They would then lead him through a reworking of the scene. The actor playing Amelia would be the anchor.

You should find it quite easy in a scripted Forum to mark up the salient points that you want the audience to notice.

On arrival on site you should meet up with the other actor (if you haven't travelled to the venue with them) and the actual facilitator, if there is one, and check exactly which points are the ones that you feel need bringing out.

You will begin the session as actor/facilitator by giving a short introduction to the audience. If you're using a scripted piece, then you probably don't need to explain all the ins and outs of Forum Theatre at this point. You can just get on and explain the situation. In this instance you might say:

> 'Good afternoon. We are here today to look at
> techniques one might use when networking on behalf
> of one's firm at social events. Let's take a look at the
> young lawyer Miles, that's me, and how he networks
> at a drinks party with a potential client. You might
> just want to make a note of anything that Miles does
> that you think is particularly effective or not.'

At this point go straight into the scene. The second actor (the anchor) doesn't really need to be introduced, as the scene will do that for you. With this sort of scripted scene you can play it out and, dare I say it, play it up a little. Enjoy it and hopefully the audience will enjoy it too. Obviously you will sense how the scene is going down, which will be a good guide as to how you play the transition.

At the end of the scene the second actor should just take a step back and you as the actor/facilitator can turn to the audience and ask: 'How did I do?' – meaning, of course, 'How did Miles do?' You may be faced with a rush of comments pointing out exactly what you did wrong! More likely you'll be faced with silence. The people in the room may not know that they have to engage with you, and some of them may be nervous of the fact that you're an actor, so they may be refraining from doing so. After all, they will probably have seen Derren Brown pick a volunteer out of the audience so they think they know what happens!

If it is proving difficult, you can make the question you're asking more specific. 'Did I do anything well?' You will know from your work with the facilitator as to what the good behaviours exhibited in that script were. There are very few, but you could point out that:

1.   You did manage to try and sell your firm.

2.   You did at least manage to bring a business card, even if it was out of date.

Then you can ask the audience for examples of what you didn't do so well. There should be more response here. People find it easier to take the opportunity to criticise. Accept a few of the comments and then start to get the Forum Theatre moving.

Tell the audience that you're going to have the meeting with Amelia again. This time you're going to ask them to help you get through the encounter more effectively. You can explain to the audience what you'd like them to do.

> 'If you see me do anything that you don't like, that you don't think is effective, or that could be done in a way that will get better results, please just shout out.'

Getting the audience to call out works if the group isn't too large. From personal experience I would say that if you're playing the forum to a group of more than fifteen or so people, then it's probably best to ask them to put their hands up, otherwise you can get drowned out by too many interruptions and never move the scene forward.

You also have the option of taking a 'time-out' yourself when you approach a tricky point in the conversation. Rather than go ahead and make the next mistake, you might take a time-out, turn to the audience and ask them: 'I'm not really sure what to do here.'

You will find it is quite a good technique to use if the audience have been stopping you a great number of times, as it can get them on your side. Listen to a number of suggestions from the audience, and then you can make your choice. You should probably choose a suggestion that you know will work well. Turn back into the scene and continue.

On a scripted Forum you can start the reworking of the scene by using the script again, but as the audience will be offering suggestions, both actors should be prepared to depart from the script quite quickly.

Start the scene again, either from the script, or in an improvisational form, and make sure there's a very big error made on your part very early on. In this scene you can do this by interrupting Amelia almost immediatly.

Hopefully you will have provoked somebody into shouting out or putting up their hand. If not, a line or so after the interruption, you can turn to the audience taking your own 'time-out' and say: 'Are you liking everything?'

Let's take the best situation here. You've just been interrupted and the audience are calling out for you to stop the scene. Stop the scene, and turn out to face the audience. You might find it useful to take one or two paces away from where you've been playing the scene in order to make it clear that now you are in facilitator mode. Ask the audience what the problem is. They'll probably tell you that you shouldn't have interrupted and should have listened to what Amelia had to say. You can acknowledge this and say that you're going to give it a try. Turn back into the scene and do exactly that, so this time the second actor playing Amelia can finish her line.

The next useful point may come up when the actor playing Amelia gets to the point in the script where she says: 'We do have a few problems though.'

You as Miles carry on to say: 'No problem, we can solve that.' – but the audience will probably want to stop you. You may be offered advice such as: 'You need to investigate that.' Or: 'Get her to tell you more.'

The various solutions that they offer to you are what make up the Forum. There may be debates in the room as to what is the best way to proceed. You as actor/facilitator need to manage this debate, make sure that people are getting their say, and aim to move it forward as cleanly and as clearly as possible. You may then take a potential solution from one member of the audience and decide to work with it.

This is the point at which the real strength of Forum Theatre comes into play. You shouldn't just follow their instructions in a general sense. You need them to be specific. You need them to give you *the actual line* that you will say. I always explain at this point that of course:

> 'I'm just an actor. I work best with lines. It really helps
> if you give me the words that will let me do what you
> would like me to do.'

If they're telling you to investigate more, then ask them to give you the line of dialogue that will enable you to do that. It might be a question such as: 'Would you tell me a little more about that?' Remember what we have said earlier. You are not a solution provider. You are there to create a situation that will facilitate learning. You should work with the person in the audience so as to get them to give you the line. They may now say: 'You should be saying to her, "What sort of problems are you encountering?"'

You can check with the rest of the audience as to whether they like this line, if you feel that this is indeed a good way to move things forward. Be careful that you don't get into a debate at this point. You can try the line and see the results.

It's the job of the second actor to know what accepted good practice is in the situation you are demonstrating. To ask an investigative question such as those suggested by the audience is a good thing in networking, so at this point the actor playing Amelia would reward you with more information about what the problem is that she is facing during the corporate restructure.

It's your decision as the actor/facilitator as to how many 'mistakes and errors' you make for the audience to pick up on. Sometimes, of course, they will pick up on things that you didn't realise they were going to stop you on. You should acknowledge these and get advice from the audience as to how to move forward, but if you don't feel it is a major learning point, don't allow it to take up too much time.

As the Forum progresses you should display more and more positive behaviours so that the gaps between interruptions become longer.

You should also be aware of the time. You will have been given a time limit for the Forum, and it's the job of both actors to time manage so that the scene and an effective conclusion fit within the appointed duration of the session.

At base level, the second actor only has to respond 'in role'. Sometimes, though, the audience might be keen to know how they're feeling as a result of what was said. It can be very effective for you to ask the second actor for some in character feedback.

For example, in the scene we have been working on, you might ask Amelia how she felt when she was interrupted and constantly told that Miles's firm could do the work. The second actor knows that interruptions are not positive and that telling people you can do the work without investigating what work is to be done is also not good practice. The second actor might respond in character saying: 'I didn't feel as though I was being listened to, and therefore I really didn't want to have to stay in the conversation with him.'

The main thing for the actor/facilitator is that you remain in charge. You should feel comfortable with what would be the right behaviour in the situation that you are demonstrating in Forum.

At the end of the Forum, when Miles and Amelia have had their successful meeting, it's always good for the actor/facilitator to acknowledge and thank the audience. Make sure that you also draw out some learning points. You can get the audience to do this by asking people to identify good behaviours or practices that you have been incorporated into the scene thanks to their guidance.

You as actor/facilitator should align yourself with the audience as closely as possible. You should be able to get the audience working as a team to come up with good suggestions that you can put into practice.

Unscripted Forum Theatre

Not all Forums are scripted and for many Forum Theatre sessions you will just be given a brief, a situation, which you and the other actor will turn into a scene. This is most often used where the learning for the audience is less based on rules and regulations, such as diversity policy, and more aimed at generic skills, such as listening and questioning. Often the scenario might be given to you by the facilitator who will then leave you to come up with the scene.

One particular example of an unscripted Forum I remember, is being asked to be a manager who had to interview a member of their team who had personal-hygiene issues. Putting aside the obvious comedy potential, the key points that the original scene had to get across were the ability of the manager to question gently, to explore the answers, and to listen. Quite often unscripted Forums can be based on issues that have actually occurred.

So the starting point is for you and your fellow actor to create the original scene from improvisation. Don't rehearse it line by line. This is a time where trust in the person you are working with is key. The best and most realistic Forum scenes are where the actors launch into it, well prepared regarding content, but totally prepared to find the dialogue moment by moment. Just talk through the general layout of the scene and how you think it might run. You both need to be sure what practices you are going to demonstrate during the scene, i.e. what deliberate mistakes you're going to make.

There is a school of thought within Forum Theatre – and it's one that I tend to subscribe to – which says that if the opening scene is so full of horrendous, horrible and obvious mistakes, the tone of the event can become rather patronising to the audience. A little bit like some of those training films from the 1950s and '60s where people made stupidly obvious errors. It was hard to believe they would happen in real life.

For example, in the Forum referred to above, it would be a little obvious for the manager to open the scene with the line: 'Have a seat, Jean. Now I need to discuss why you smell!'

It might bring the house down, but in no way would be believable as the behaviour of a manager.

So, in creating the scenario for the unscripted Forum Theatre, you as actors want to get a balance between believable realism and demonstrating bad practice, so that the audience will accept you and want to help you.

On some courses, mainly owing to time constraints, when you are working in an unscripted Forum, you may be asked not to do the full scene to start with, but to explain how Forum Theatre works at the beginning of the session and plunge straight into the scene where the audience will help you.

In this case, you have to make sure you explain the rules of Forum Theatre very clearly and that the audience acknowledge that they understand them.

You as the actor/facilitator should then be looking for an interruption within the first thirty seconds of the scene. This might be a moment to demonstrate a piece of bad practice, but not so glaringly obvious in its execution that even the newest and greenest graduate couldn't but fail to notice it. Good examples of noticeable bad practice are interrupting as soon as the other person speaks, or using phrases such as: 'Yes, I hear you, but what I wanted to say…'

This is to ensure that the audience understand the process and use it to the full. You and your fellow actor are in charge of that process, and it is your job to ensure that it works. You have to understand what good and bad practice in the situation is, but you don't have to point it out to the audience. You use the Forum techniques to let them see how good practice works. If they come up with the solution and you execute it, they will remember it much better.

You should also be aware that some people will like the whole process of Forum Theatre a great deal. They'll like it so much that they will not be able to resist calling out. They will even like it so much that they won't be able to resist calling out all the time at every possible opportunity. Your job as actor/facilitator is to make sure that any such dominant personalities do not take over the whole group, but that you receive suggestions from as many people as possible.

Particularly early on in the process, make sure that you don't block too many suggestions. The more suggestions you seem prepared to accept and try out, the more suggestions the audience will give you.

The role of the second actor in an unscripted Forum Theatre is simpler but no less important. The second actor, or anchor as we have referred to them, stays in character throughout. As the anchor you must know the whole of the role-play brief equally well. You should know what good practice is in the area that you are dealing with, and it will be up to you to let the role-play move forward. If you feel that the suggestion the audience gave your actor/facilitator (and that he is putting into practice), is a good one, then you can allow the role-play to move forward. You can block suggestions that you know to be bad practice.

You will never relate directly to the audience as the anchor. Even if you're asked what your feelings are at a particular time, or following a particular question, you shouldn't engage in any conversation with the audience. Use the rules of feedback just as you would in a one-to-one role-play, and feed back to the actor/facilitator in that fashion.

> 'When you asked me that question, I felt confused as you didn't wait for my answer.'

Can I Have a Volunteer?

One of the advantages of Forum Theatre is that it can be used with large audiences, who can enjoy the comfortable anonymity of the crowd thinking they're not going to be involved. It's often used when people have expressed dislike of role-play. But as the Forum proceeds, you, as the actor/facilitator, will inevitably build up a rapport with your audience. They will find themselves drawn in. They will become involved and they will start offering some quite complicated suggestions. When you ask them for the words that you should say, you can sometimes receive an extremely loquacious monologue in reply.

If you feel that that particular audience member is up for it, you can say: 'I can't possibly remember all that. Why don't you come up here and give it a try?' You might meet some resistance. In fact, of course, you will meet some resistance. Unless they are budding contestants on *Britain's Got Talent*, no one really relishes the opportunity to get up in front of their peers and colleagues to demonstrate best practice. Yet if the suggestion is genuinely a good one, a little light pressure will soon get the person to come up to the front and sit in your chair.

Let them do the line and let the role-play run for thirty seconds to one minute afterwards. Keep an eye on them and check they are okay, and when you stop the role-play make sure you lead the response with something positive. Applause is the most obvious, but a big 'Well done!' will also help.

If their suggestion was good and worked well, make sure you bring out the learning points from their time in the chair.

If you are the anchor, make sure you give a positive response to the participant's line. The actor/facilitator should have only let them sit in the chair if their suggestion was one in accordance with good practice. If they continue on in the role-play following your response, then you can challenge them gently. Remember they are on show in front of many of their colleagues and, ideally, you don't want to allow them to fail.

Getting a volunteer to join a Forum can be exceptionally effective. You need to be sure you have the right person. You need to be sure they've made a positive good practice suggestion. You need to manage their involvement and end it with positive feedback and response. You need to make sure that they have a good time sitting in the chair. If they feel good about it, they will take that feeling away with them. And so will the audience.

Humour

Humour in any Forum Theatre situation can be particularly effective. You will have a large audience. There is much more of an element of a show about this style of work. Sometimes the temptation to get a quick, funny, topical reference into the scene can be overwhelming.

Your guideline should be: never aim for humour at the expense of content. Sometimes your audience will come up with some great suggestions that can be played into the Forum Theatre scenario for good comic effect. One of the best I remember was when I played a manager dealing with a personal assistant who was finding her workload difficult. She was on the verge of tears. The actress playing opposite me seemed to be getting a lot of sympathy. Suddenly from the audience came the suggestion: 'Tell her to man up or she's fired!' Not the most empathetic of responses perhaps, and certainly one that the group thought was probably not worth trying. Yet the person who had given the suggestion was insistent I try it. I used the line exactly as I had been given it. The actress concerned came back with a delightfully shocked yet low-key reaction that she slowly built up into a fit of hysterics and tears to something worthy of the third act of *Titus Andronicus*. Exceptionally entertaining, very funny, and yet we also managed to bring out the learning point that direct talk at such a time was not what was needed.

Working with a Separate Facilitator

You may find that you arrive to do a Forum Theatre session, scripted or not, with another actor, to be told by the facilitator who is running the course that they will be taking part. This will very likely change the relationship of the actor/facilitator to the audience.

The main thing is for the three of you to establish your own working rules before the Forum Theatre session commences. One good way that you can make it work is as follows.

The facilitator can introduce the session and explain how the forum will work. They can then hand over to you, the actor/facilitator, to explain your role and the issue that you will be dealing with. You can also explain who the person you will be meeting is. This is preferable to the second actor coming out of character and introducing themselves. It is much more effective for the second actor to stay in character throughout.

You can start the Forum as you would normally, but as soon as you get to an issue where either the audience stops you, or you take a time-out, you should turn to the facilitator, explain the problem to them and then let them deal with the interaction with the audience.

You may find this frustrating, as it's more than likely that the facilitator will have absolutely no theatrical instincts whatsoever. You may hear some very good suggestions coming up that would have allowed for some fun exploration. But the facilitator, who is solely focused on what is called good practice in the issue you're dealing with, may well only be looking for suggestions that they feel are positive and will move the issue forward.

In spite of the fact that they have missed a couple of suggestions that would have enabled you to come up with something almost as hysterical as the last ten minutes of *Run for Your Wife*, you need to hold back and wait until the facilitator turns to you with the suggestion that they want you to play. Make sure that the facilitator gives you the line, and doesn't turn the audience suggestion into something non-specific like: 'Could you be a little more empathetic?' Other than that, let the facilitator deal with the audience.

I have to say that having an external facilitator isn't as much fun as when you're allowed to do it for yourself, but they may be an expert on the issue and have far more information at their fingertips than you. It also allows them to play a useful part in the session and helps them not to feel undermined by the actors.

Grin and bear it.

Timekeeping

Forum Theatre sessions can vary in length, so it is vital that you check with the facilitator or client before you start as to just how long you have. Make sure both actors are aware of this. It might be a good idea to synchronise your watches, assuming that both of you are wearing watches, or to check whether there is a clock in the room that you can both see.

Forty-five minutes is a good length of time for a Forum Theatre session to deal with one issue. You should be aiming to work through the whole scenario within that time.

It can be incredibly frustrating for everyone when the Forum Theatre is going really well, and you're dealing with lots of good suggestions, for a facilitator to step in and say: 'Well, I'm afraid we're going to have to leave it there for time reasons.' It can leave the group feeling unfulfilled, which in turn undermines the good work that you have done during the session.

Probably the best person to manage the time is the anchor – the actor who has remained in character throughout. There will be a lot of times the actor/facilitator is dealing with the audience, when, as anchor, and the slightly less involved actor (although, of course, you will be listening to all the suggestions that are being made), you can steal a quick glance at your watch. If need be, you can then help by speeding up the progress of the scene.

Ideally you want to wrap up a Forum Theatre session five minutes before the time limit so that you can ask the audience to sum up some of the learning points. If you get the audience to tell you what they've learnt, they then know what they're taking away from the session.

Good timekeeping is part of good role-play. Quite often the Forum Theatre session is only one part of a busy and heavily timetabled day. Bringing it in on time will leave you with happy clients and hopefully further bookings.

Summary

- Used for larger audiences.
- May be used in situations where people are frightened of role-play
- Two kinds of Forum Theatre: scripted and unscripted.
- Two forms of performance: one with a complete scene at the beginning; one going straight into the interactive.
- Two roles: the actor/facilitator and the anchor.
- Make sure the rules are clear for the audience.
- Try to ensure that you get an audience interruption within thirty seconds of the start of the scene.
- Remember, you're not there to give the solutions.
- Ask the audience to give you the line you have to say next.
- Don't let dominant members of the group take over.
- Keep things moving forward.
- Finish with a few minutes left to sum up and conclude.
- Highlight the learning points in your summary.

❝ I remember doing a diversity job for a large corporate banking client: four actors, and three Forums, looking at workplace behaviours. This session had been commissioned and delivered across all the bank's population over a number of years, and was expressly designed to address respect in the workplace, the acceptance of difference, unconscious bias, etc. All the scenes were set in a parallel mythical organisation, which nonetheless exactly mirrored the behaviours and attitudes revealed during interviews with the bank's staff.

In the first Forum, I played a young front-office trader, happy to exploit anyone and anything in his quest for success. On this occasion the participants were sixty new joiners, both front and back office, mainly drawn from the firm's graduate training programme. They were an enthusiastic crowd, who enjoyed challenging the characters on their interpersonal behaviours and attitudes.

Having played out the scene, we as characters were then questioned by the audience about the motivations behind our behaviours, given feedback on our actions and then offered advice as to how to operate more successfully in future.

Our facilitator asked if there was any advice for my character. One particularly extrovert individual told me that my tie (which was indeed pink) was a clear signal that I must be gay, and if I wanted to progress in the firm I should rethink my wardrobe...

I was very thrown by the comment. My character was definitely straight, and indeed had expressed quite a few inappropriate remarks to that end during the scene, but as a gay man myself it went immediately to my own feelings of self. Had I not been 'straight enough'? Am I transparently gay, whatever that means? I felt myself blush, and my mind raced as I thought of how to respond to what felt like a very public challenge to the character, the programme and to me.

And then I remembered the golden rule of facilitation: the answer is always out there. Still in character, I responded by asking him to tell me more about why he thought a pink tie meant I might be gay? Clearly embarrassed, our participant gave no meaningful response. I then opened it up to the rest of the room by asking: 'What does anyone else think?' The other participants disagreed publicly, debated and challenged his thought process. Equilibrium was restored. This was the learning for him and for them. After the session, he came and apologised, saying he was just trying to crack a joke, but having reflected he could see why it was inappropriate.

Drama-based training isn't about providing the answers, lecturing about behaviours or telling participants what to think. It is about providing a space for people to express their opinions and debate amongst themselves the most appropriate way forward, however uncomfortable it can sometimes feel. It's not about us and what we think. It's about them.

Toby Sawyer

7

Live Events…

And How to Escape with Your Dignity Intact

We have all done it.

We've been walking through a busy shopping centre on a day off or at the weekend with our families, and coming towards us, brandishing a promotional leaflet, is a large furry something. It could be a bright-yellow duck, a large pink sausage in a bread roll, or a rather animated bottle of washing-up liquid. Whatever it is, the same thought goes through your head: 'Bet there is a poor bloody actor inside there!'

And you're probably right. There is.

This represents the very bottom level of the live-events market. It's probably the area of the corporate world where most of the horror stories come from. It's certainly the sector of the corporate market where, having been brought in to do a particular job, you may be asked to do something that requires none of your skills in particular, but a whole different level of chutzpah that sometimes only actors are poor and desperate enough to provide.

I want to take a quick look at some of the different areas in which actors can be used, and how to protect yourself against the possible pitfalls.

Exhibition Work

I'm a bit of a gadget freak, and if you combine that with anything that helps me in the kitchen, then it's not at all surprising that most years I tend to make a beeline for the Ideal Home Show. I am usually lucky in persuading a friend to accompany me for a day wandering around the stands, sitting in massage chairs, and looking at all those useful slicers, juicers, swivel-headed mops – and magnetic window cleaners that I never knew I needed. And who are the people showing me these latest wonders of budget household technology? That's right. Actors.

We often play a game of wandering round the exhibition to give an award for the person we feel is doing the most energetic presentation in the circumstances.

This year I had an actor make me an omelette in a new-style, double-hinged frying pan. I had an actor place my stockinged feet in a foot massager. And my good friend Harriet had an actress style her hair with a supposedly amazing new scrunchie!

For that's what you will be doing if you go into the world of exhibitions. Presenting on an almost continuous basis. It's a little like cinema performances used to be when I was a child. A double-bill would be advertised as 'continuous performances'. The cinema would open around ten past twelve in the afternoon and show the first film. It would then continue to show both films one after the other all day with just a five-minute gap between each one while the projectionist changed the reels. People quite often arrived at a time that they chose and watched the two films round until they arrived at the point where they could declare: 'This is where we came in', and leave.

At an exhibition, you can give literally hundreds of performances a day. A short three- to four-minute product presentation could be repeated fifteen times an hour in an eight-hour day. Or you could also be fronting a stand at a larger exhibition in a more specialist market such as IT, communications technology or media information, where major players such as Samsung, Sony, NEC and the rest will invest the cost of a small house in building their stand.

I once worked for a Japanese technology company at an exhibition in Geneva in Switzerland. The stand we were working on was a breathtaking four storeys high, with private lounges, meeting rooms, kitchens and changing rooms, as well as three auditoria and an exhibition area.

Having spent all this money on their stand, the client then wants to spend a disproportionately small part of money hiring an actor to do the presentation to front it.

Why hire an actor?

In general, the rates you as an actor will charge for a day's work such as this are cheaper than those of someone who calls himself a professional presenter. Given some of the presenters who currently grace our screens in 'yoof' programming, you may find it hard to believe, but yes, it's true. As an actor without a considerable television profile, you are an unknown face, which is very good from the client's point of view as you are purely an information giver, but one who can also add emotion and feeling to what can often be a very dry, informative script. And all at a very economical rate.

One of the key things to find out when offered such work is just how many shows a day you will be expected to do. What will be your break arrangements? What are the working hours on show days?

I regularly used to present and direct a presentation for Lotus IBM that would play at two exhibitions each year. The show days, which were usually three or four in a row, would begin with the first show at ten in the morning and then the shows would continue at half-hour intervals with the last show kicking off at five in the afternoon. That's fifteen shows a day.

The shows would be about twenty minutes in length, so technically at the end of each show there was an eight-to-ten minute turnaround before the next one started. It would be a particularly unrealistic client or production company that expected one actor to deliver all these presentations. Quite often we would have two teams. One team would deliver the first three presentations of the day, and then go off on an hour's break while the second team took over. Even with the breaks it can be pretty exhausting work. Not all stands have executive resting lounges, and even if they do you can almost guarantee that one will not be provided for the use of the actors.

You should probably enquire as to what changing facilities there are and expect that the answer will almost certainly be 'none'. Or you may be shown a room with a little 'male' or 'female' sign on the door, and you would be right in thinking it is the public toilet. Don't use it. You might be expected to put on your suit, or costume if you're particularly unlucky, at the hotel and arrive for work in it. This can mean that you have to spend your break attired for the show. Double-check that there is somewhere you can take off the comedy duck costume so that you can have your lunch looking like a human being.

I have done whole days presenting at technology exhibitions at the RAI in Amsterdam where there have not been two presenters and I have been expected to give an eighteen-minute presentation every half an hour. In these instances, you should pre-negotiate your lunch-break arrangements. You will also find it helpful if you make absolutely sure that someone is there to provide tea and coffee for you in the very short break you have between each show.

Locate the nearest toilet. In places like Earls Court and the NEC, the walk to the nearest toilet can often take five minutes. A return trip could occupy the whole of your break between presentations.

Working with a script

These repeat presentations, no matter how they are dressed up, will nearly always be selling some sort of product, software, or concept. As such, the job will probably demand that you work from quite a tight script. The marketing department may well have worked long and hard on considering what you should say.

You should ask about the script when accepting the job and when negotiating the rate for the day. You may not be given an opportunity to negotiate the daily rate for the job. You can be sure, however, that the client will not have factored in any learning time for the script. Do this now.

It can take several days' hard work to learn an eighteen-to twenty-minute script off by heart. People who never have to learn scripts have no concept of the amount of time it can take, and how to do it. The fact is that you really need to have an emotional connection to learn a whole set of lines – which you can guarantee you won't have if you're selling the latest digital-media transfer giga-byte selector or whatever it is. It will just be learning six, seven, or eight pages off by heart, parrot fashion. And that is hard work! It is certainly something you as an actor can do, but it is not something you as an actor can do easily, and it will take time. This time should be costed into the equation.

I generally look at a script and ask for a day or two's fee to learn it. In fact, it can often take a week or more to learn a long script. Remember that when you deliver the script you'll have to look confident, assured, and give the appearance of knowing what you're talking about. You will not have been through a full rehearsal process. In some instances, you may only have had the chance to run the script once or twice in situ before starting to deliver it to the public visiting the exhibition.

Once I was given an eighteen-page script on digital-media transfer to learn. I understood absolutely nothing about it, and I spent ten long evenings learning it, parrot fashion, to deliver on the stand. At a very quick rehearsal on the day before the exhibition opened, I was allowed to run through the script on the stand with a visual presentation playing on the screen behind me. Workmen were still hammering in nails and assembling various exhibition elements, but with a mammoth effort of concentration I got from beginning to end. I have to say I was very pleased with myself.

At this point someone from the client approached the person who was in charge of the presentation and pointed out that there were several errors in the script. In fact, there were quite a lot of errors. Not simple grammatical errors, but nearly all of the numbers needed changing. A meeting was held by the client and at 5.30 p.m. I was presented with a new eighteen-page script with virtually every number changed. 1.27 GB had become 2.13 GB. 37 megahertz were now 55 megahertz. And so on. I had to point out that relearning this script by 10 a.m. was just not going to happen, and that if they wanted it presented with all the new figures in place, I would have to work from cue cards with the script pasted onto them. They looked at me with blank incomprehension, and reluctantly they agreed. They didn't really understand why it wasn't possible for me to change all the numbers in the script just as easily as they had changed them.

I know that you understand.

To learn a script to which you have no emotional connection, and which you are just learning 'dry', is probably one of the hardest things you will ever be asked to do as an actor. You will all have your own methods. You do, however, have to be realistic, and it was clear to me that it was entirely unrealistic to expect me to deliver that new script the following morning.

I worked from cue cards for the whole of the following day. Funnily enough, by the end of the day on Friday, having delivered the new script fourteen times, I was alarmingly familiar with it.

You just need to make sure that the client doesn't have unrealistic expectations of you as an actor.

On the other hand, don't be difficult. Work to the best of your ability, and keep an open dialogue with whoever is managing you on behalf of the client. Remember, you are their shop window. You are their brand. They are trusting in you at a major sales opportunity for their company. They need it to work.

Sometimes, though, what happens will be beyond your control. Particularly in the technological areas, what you might be demonstrating or showing to the public could well be a prototype or what is known as a 'beta'. This means that the product works in theory. In practice, things might not go as smoothly as you would like.

Janet Ellis, the television presenter and a long-standing friend of mine, remembers this:

“ Some time in the mid-'90s I was press-ganged by my good friend and colleague Paul Clayton into playing the role of a television host on a fictitious programme called *Good Morning with Pam and Dick* at a software fair in a Heathrow hotel.

Using the format of a morning-television chat show, Paul and I were presenting a couple of new ideas in the software field. One of these was the extremely ambitious for its time, 'Simply Speaking', a voice-to-text programme for computers.

This was being demonstrated by a lovely lady called Pam. Pam came from Liverpool and she had invested many hours in training the software to recognise her voice and to show her words on screen as she spoke. As we watched the programme during rehearsals we were all incredibly impressed. The gentle lilt of her scouse was translated into perfect sentences on the screen.

Our first show was at ten on a Saturday morning. All was going unbelievably smoothly as I invited Pam to join us 'in the studio'.

I think it might have been the nerves of suddenly standing in front of an audience of a hundred or so people that got to the lovely Pam. I'm not sure, but something certainly happened to her voice. It rose just a little in tone and pitch, and the software started to have problems identifying what she was saying.

She dictated to the machine: 'It's good to be here on a Saturday morning', and to my horror on the screen behind me, the computer decided to print out the phrase 'anti-Semitic Nazis at Tesco'.

There is not much you can do in such circumstances other than smile. The audience were hooting, and the ever-reliable Mr Clayton was curled up at the side of the stage on a sofa in paroxysms of delight. With what I hope was a reasonable degree of professionalism, I thanked Pam and brought the item to a swift and somewhat premature conclusion.

I should just point out that that was over sixteen years ago, and I have dictated most of this book using a similar programme, so things really do get much better.

Summary

Here are the questions you need to ask:

- How long is the presentation?
- How many presentations are there in each day?
- What are my breaks?
- What are the costume requirements?

… And, of course:

- What is the fee?

It's amazing how often you will find that one element of the above information is missing.

About ten years ago, my good friend and colleague Brian Jordan and I were booked for five days at a computer-games exhibition at Earls Court in London. A corporate agent had sold us to the client as experienced corporate presenters who could improvise and work without a script.

Alarm bells began to ring very slightly when we were sent to Angels the costumiers to organise for ourselves some Arabian Grand Vizier costumes! After ninety minutes we left having bedecked ourselves as two renegades from Disney's *Aladdin*.

We turned up early on a Sunday morning and found the stand. A mini Arabian palace had been built to promote the game *Prince of Persia 2*. The ground floor consisted of several games consoles where people could try out a level of the new game, and upstairs there were minarets and a balcony on which we were to work. We had spent our journey there discussing good Arabian gags, and possible material, but up on the balcony, there was no sound system. No one had thought that our 'witty themed banter' would need to be heard.

As soon as the exhibition opened it became clear that no one at all was interested in engaging with two rather strange and very English characters on the upper level. They wanted to see the game, and they wanted to get a T-shirt. That's what exhibitions are about for many people. Collecting as many goodie bags and T-shirts as they can.

Our duties very quickly changed to throwing T-shirts from the upper level every two minutes or so in order to pull a crowd to the stand. They couldn't hear what we were saying, and it was pointless trying to engage them. Suffice it to say that it wasn't what we had signed up for and, indeed, for two people to throw T-shirts to a baying crowd, the client had paid a great deal of money. We went home at the end of day one. I rang two other younger actors who needed the money, and we sent them along the next day having first cleared it with the producer.

So always make sure what it is that you will be doing.

Money

It's always difficult to talk about money.

There are no set rates for this sort of work, no Equity guide-lines in place, and the rates offered can vary enormously.

If you are approached by a corporate agent or a production company with a piece of work, then quite often you might be asked what your daily rate is. At this point it is essential to know just how many shows you will be doing, how long the day will be and all the other vital information that I have already highlighted.

As a rough guide, in 2012, a good daily rate for seven to eight hours of rolling presentations is around £750–£800 a day. It's perfectly possible to achieve this rate if you are the main presenter on the stand and have a script to learn as well.

I charge rehearsal days and learning days at half the presentation-day rate. In addition, the greater the number of days the client buys, the lower the rate becomes. For example, if they were to buy two days of eight shows a day, I would want to charge a minimum of £800 a day. I would charge £400 for a rehearsal day, and £400 for learning the script. If, however, the number of show days were to rise to five, then I would offer to reduce the daily show rate to £750 or even £700.

You need to know what your higher and lower daily rates are. This has to be based on your experience, your saleabil-ity, and your suitability for the job. For example, if you're one of only four actors who have an in-depth knowledge of digital-media fat-reduction techniques and this is key to the job, then you can command a higher rate than if the work merely requires reading an autocue and looking good.

Once you've got a picture of what's involved, ask the person offering the job what sort of money they have. If that equates with roughly what you are thinking is a good daily rate, then all well and good. You could always ask for just a little bit more, as no client worth their salt will have put all their money on the table on the first offer, but be reasonable. Don't out-price yourself, but don't underprice yourself either. If you feel the fee that is offered is fair, then take it.

The fees I am talking about here are for the main presenter on an exhibition stand. Jobs such as handing out T-shirts, leaflets, etc., are all really priced at promotional-work level, which is much lower (see below).

Remember that the negotiation could be the beginning of a long relationship with the client. If you're not doing it through an agent, then be honest, be friendly and be as open and up front as you can.

Also remember that if you are getting the job through a corporate agent and pricing yourself at £500 a day, you can be reasonably sure that the client is paying around £650–£700 a day for you. So that's what they'll be thinking you cost and that's what you have to live up to.

Promotional Work

A lot of exhibition work is promotion-based. You are selling or demonstrating a product or service at a particular level. But it's not only at exhibitions that this sort of work is available.

One Saturday while writing this book, my partner and I were making our normal circuitous journey around the aisles in our local Waitrose. On turning into the chilled-foods section, we found an actor promoting a new form of 'pour and chill it yourself' crème brulée. So there we were shopping, and there's an actor earning a living in the corporate world.

There are a lot of agencies that employ actors, models and dancers to do promotional work. You can google them quite easily, but ones that come to mind immediately are Staff Live, The Field, Kru Live and ID Staffing. Their websites are easy to find, and on several of them you can register for an interview or audition via the web.

I spoke to the actor I met in Waitrose at greater length over a coffee. He had completed a one-year postgraduate course in acting at The Drama Studio and left in the middle of 2011. He'd had the normal run of fringe appearances and some small-scale unpaid film work, but it's the promotional work that has paid the bills and kept him going through this first year out of training.

You should appreciate that this sort of work can bring dizzying heights and terrifying lows. I'd never considered that standing in the cold-food aisle of Waitrose for eight hours could be unpleasant, but then I've never had cause to spend that amount of time in a supermarket. If I were out filming in the cold for eight hours, I'd make sure I had decent thermals and that was the case here too. Good preparation on the part of the actor.

To be successful in promotional work, you have got to be friendly, personable and responsible. You should be a good timekeeper and able to cope with the vagaries of the British public at large. You could find yourself, as indeed one actor did, dressed as a giant yeti promoting a car manufacturer at Wembley for an England international. You might find it starts off well with fans happy to have their picture taken with you, but as the fans get merrier and more raucous, you could find that inside a yeti costume is a very vulnerable place to be. No harm came to the actor concerned, but there was probably a severe loss of dignity as he was buffeted around by discontented fans and lost his head (quite literally) on several occasions.

You can find yourself mixing with celebrities and the glitterati at promotional launches. Another actor I know recently took an Xbox stand into a hall in Victoria for MPs to come and play on at a promotional event. Watching the leaders of the coalition unite as the Mario Bros is a privilege denied to most of us.

You will find that the notice given you for jobs in the promotional world varies a great deal. A phone call can come from an agency the night before, and sometimes they can book you a month in advance. Actors have spoken of occasions where they've been rung first thing in the morning and asked if they were free for the rest of the day. This is great. These sorts of very short-notice bookings are hardly likely to clash with auditions and interviews. These are the exception. More of a problem is what to do when you have an advance booking for some promotional work and your acting agent rings with an interview or audition.

Let the corporate or promotional agency have as much notice as possible. If you're cancelling a job that they are going to find very difficult to cover, you can't expect them to ring you again and offer you more work. The actor I spoke to in Waitrose, who was on the books of several corporate promotional agencies, had, in fact, been suspended by one of them, as he had had to cancel a number of jobs over recent weeks owing to interviews and castings.

If they can't replace you on the promotional work, then you have to weigh up the advantages of having regular work, or taking the risk of losing further corporate work and go for the interview. This can depend on your relationship with the booker at the agency, so explore it at the time of booking. Ask what sort of notice they would need if you were to cancel. Some jobs have actors on them who are specially trained for that job, and the agency may only have a few of you. If that's the case then cancelling is more difficult, but on the plus side you are probably getting a higher rate of pay for that sort of job in the first place.

Promotional work tends to pay around £60 a day, and the hours can vary from three or four hours to a full eight-hour day. Bear that in mind if you're going to be standing next to a chiller cabinet!

The money goes up if you take on additional responsibilities and become an event manager. Something up to the £120-a-day mark. This can involve leading a team who are out on the road promoting anything from soft drinks to cleaning fluid, and can involve a certain amount of paperwork. Bear in mind that some jobs can involve you doing some prep work before the day. My Waitrose actor, for example, was responsible for making up the samples of crème brulée himself each night before the next day's work. Since this could consist of eight trays of one hundred and forty cups per tray, that's quite a bit of preparation work which you need to factor in.

Promotional actors usually work in their own clothes, and as the work involves a lot of standing you'll need a good pair of comfortable shoes. The agency or the client will normally provide T-shirts or hoodies for you to work in.

You can amass several days of this sort of work each month, and most agencies tend to pay you at the end of the month following the one you did the work in. So all your work in July would be paid at the end of August. You'd need to factor this into your budgeting, as this can include your travel expenses for getting to and from the job. Sometimes this can involve you in a fair amount of travel. It would not be unusual for London-based actors to be sent to Southend or Brighton for the day on this sort of work.

People who do best in this field are the people who have great energy, and manage to maintain a relationship with the agents they are working for as well as the public.

A Promotional Agent Speaks

This is all born out by an interview I had with Tom Eaten-ton, Managing Director of Kru Live, one of the largest and most sought-after providers of promotional and event staff.

How many actors does your company use during a year?

In an average year we use a large number of actors. In percentage terms, that can be thousands of people. Forty per cent of our staff would be actors across the UK, and that can rise as high as sixty per cent for events based in London.

What are the skills that make actors suitable for your work?

By definition, actors can perform and 'act up'. The face-to-face nature of our business is such that people with outgoing, lively and enthusiastic personalities are perfect for it. They are able to engage and interest those people our clients market to and create 'theatre' to make the encounter memorable.

What most irritates you about actors who work for you?

Without a doubt the major downside to the industry and agency booking teams is reliability. Actors seem to perceive this work as secondary to their primary passion and career. To a degree you can understand it; but there are very few that remember 'life' is about making commitments and following through with them. Far too often actors will agree and commit to a booking, and we will send their details and profile cards to clients who will approve and invite them on to their teams, sometimes getting as far as investing in costly training, only to be let down the day before the event, or on dates throughout a campaign, owing to an audition or part that has come up. We completely understand the need for actors to audition, but many seem to forget the impact a last-minute cancellation has on our reputation and long-term relationships with clients. Our rule is, once you have committed and agreed to an activity or event with us and want to be booked regularly with us, then you need to see it through. We will always do our best to replace people so they can attend important castings, auditions or roles, but if not possible we do ask that they follow through with the booking agreed with us.

Do actors tend to get booked and rebooked by your account managers for doing a good job?

Absolutely. People who are reliable and enthusiastic, get on well with the booking team and receive great client feedback, pretty much have their choice of work.

Having filled out a form to register, what is the next part of the process in getting work with you? An interview, audition or just a try-out?

We have an online registration form to complete first. The team will then conduct a telephone interview. Following this, an invite will be sent for either a one-on-one interview, a group interview, or a recruitment event.

What's more likely to get you employed in this work: looks or ability?

There is work for anyone as long as they are reliable, with a great personality and willing to work hard. Looks are important in the industry, but they aren't everything. Someone with 'model' looks that doesn't want to 'get their hands dirty' and work hard usually doesn't get requested back. Someone with a great personality and great work ethic and a well-presented appearance is always attractive to the public and the brands they represent.

So there you have it from the mouth of the employer, and it is exactly in line with the attitudes required throughout the rest of the corporate world. A sense of commitment and taking it seriously. I had the chance to see a Kru Live recruitment event, and it looked like huge fun. Challenging, entertaining and making use of an actor's skills in fun and imaginative ways, as well as testing out their ability to interact successfully with members of the public. I think it would be worth applying just to get the chance to take part in one of these workshops. It also gives people a really good idea of whether they themselves feel they would be suited to the work.

You could mark down a visit to their website as one of the things to do on your 'Get Work Plan' as detailed in Chapter 9.

Murder Evenings

This is now a huge market in the UK, and one that in its current form I have had little to do with.

Back in the early 1990s, I did prepare several corporate whodunnit evenings for major clients such as Lotus IBM, Microsoft and Hewlett Packard. Quite often they were scripted by the writers Brian Jordan or Elly Brewer, and delivered after a rehearsal, at a corporate dinner party in a restaurant, hotel or other venue.

They were not cheap to deliver. Even back then I would ensure that each actor got paid around £250 per event. That would consist of a day or a half's rehearsal, and the event itself, which could be an evening or a full day.

One of the most glamorous events we were called upon to create was a whodunnit that would last seven hours and take place on the Orient Express as it travelled from Milan to Geneva. The logistics of such an event were a nightmare. Three dining carriages each holding about thirty people, who all had to be able to witness the murder, and have an opportunity to gather evidence about all the suspects. The fact that the plot had to start at 9.00 a.m. in the morning at a hotel beside Lake Garda in Italy and end at 4.30 p.m. that afternoon in a hotel on the side of Lake Geneva in Switzerland was an added bonus, but one that entailed an enormous amount of work. We achieved the murder by arranging for the train to stop at a deserted platform at a station in Switzerland called Brig. Here at approximately 12 noon Swiss time (sorry, what do I mean 'approximately'? At *exactly* 12 noon Swiss time: what other kind of Swiss time is there?), we detrained all ninety people onto the platform and showed them a knife-throwing act that went tragically wrong. Our amateur detectives loved it. I'm still not sure to this day what the Swiss commuters on platforms one to six of Brig station thought about it. Even now the memory of the actress and choreographer Cristina Avery giving a rousing rendition of

'Me and My Shadow' amidst the lunchtime crowd at a railway station in the mountains is still one I treasure.

This was clearly an event with a large budget. Six actors, one production assistant, an original script, costumes, travel and hotel accommodation for actors all adds up. It was held by a computer company for their fifty Best European Managers. They were having a whole week on holiday at the company's expense, and our 'little whodunnit' was just a fill-in to keep them amused during the train journey on the middle day of their holiday!

In today's economic climate, you are unlikely to come across anything quite as lavish as this. On the other hand, as we have moved into the twenty-first century, murder-mystery companies run by actors have proliferated all over the country. It's not difficult to find a local hotel running a murder-mystery night three or four times a year. From my research, all would seem to be supplied by local companies, and some of them by amateurs who have broken into the market purely for this purpose.

This, of course, has driven the price down to the end client, and in return has lowered the fees available to actors for this kind of work. Whereas a big corporate whodunnit could cost between £2,000 and £3,000 ten years ago, now it's possible to hire a group of actors to perform a murder mystery for around £650. Given that the company has to take a cut of this fee, and even the smallest of the whodunnits has to have three actors (hopefully making use of that well-known plot twist, the identical twins!) you can take an informed guess at the fees now available to actors.

You will find companies out there who will pay actors £50 a night for a murder mystery. This will probably not be inclusive of travel, but check. You should also check whether the company are providing costumes, etc. They may be expecting you to mock something up from your own clothes. It's not unknown.

So what are the attributes you'll need to be part of a murder-mystery evening?

1. You'll need to be a quick learner. You will probably have scripted sections.

2. You need to be a good improviser. Many of the murder-mystery evenings involve a section where the audience are allowed to question the suspects. You'll be able to provide some of your answers from the synopsis of the plot that you've been sent, or in lucky cases, rehearsed, but the very best murder-mystery evenings rely on actors to give quick comedic responses to questions that the audience may think clever and probing.

   Lee Simpson, a founder member of the Comedy Store Players, was playing a police inspector one night and was tackled by a very keen member of the audience – a budding Poirot.

   > 'So how was the body before it went into the freezer, Inspector?'

   And with an enviable sangfroid, Mr Simpson responded:

   > 'Warmer.'

   On a murder mystery you have to respect that the audience want to be entertained, but they are keen and will be looking eagle-eyed for any loopholes in the plot. The English obsession with the country-house murder is bizarre, but it is an obsession that has kept many an actor in work on many an evening.

3. You will also need to be comfortable with working at very close quarters with members of the public. Remember the golden rule: the public will do what you least expect them to do in any given situation.

Check with the company you're working for whether the party you're going to know they are having a murder-mystery evening. For some reason, some company party planners think it's going to be great fun to surprise their colleagues with a murder mystery at a company event. It never works.

Against all our better instincts, Brian Jordan and I once accepted a booking from a firm of accountants who were holding a Christmas party at a hotel in Henley-on-Thames. The person booking the murder-mystery evening was absolutely insistent that it be kept a secret, and so we worked this into the plot. A special Chairman's Award that was going to be presented would go tragically wrong and someone would end up dead.

It became apparent within ten minutes of the group arriving at the hotel that the last thing they wanted that evening was corporate entertainment. They wanted to eat, drink, be merry and get blathered. And this they proceeded to do, while six very talented, very clever, and very funny actors died all around them in the same room. And I don't mean died in the sense of murdered!

I have to comment that this is probably not the most positive section of corporate work that I've written about. And the reason?

In my research for this book I emailed eighty murder-mystery companies listed on Google. I explained the purpose of the book, and how it would help actors looking for work in the corporate market. Not one of them agreed to an interview. I think the reason is that the sector is now so competitive, and there are so many companies fighting for what is quite a small amount of work, that they were afraid that by saying anything in interview they might be giving their competitors an edge.

You can easily google murder-mystery companies who are based near you, drop them a line and find out how they recruit their actors. If they're based on your doorstep and it is a

£50-a-night job, then it might just be worth it, but this sector of the market is not going to provide the returns you will get in role-play, in training or in conference and exhibition work.

In its own way, it could be murder!

One of my earliest experiences in the corporate world was being enrolled by the comedienne Sandi Toksvig into a project for Edge of the Seat Productions. This company no longer exists as its owner and director, Elly Brewer, has moved on to become a BAFTA award-winning television writer, but she took a moment to remind me of one of the pressures of live corporate work.

66 Think like a Boy Scout – Be Prepared...

I used to write and produce corporate theatre through my company Edge of the Seat Productions. We did a job for an upmarket office-furniture company which, for reasons which escape me now, demanded the services of one 'Paul Clayton' in character as Lady Bracknell.

Lady Bracknell's arrival was to be a secret. So I took Paul – terrifyingly gorgeous in large grey wig and whalebone corset under a floor-length Edwardian frock – off to hide in a stock cupboard until our allotted time.

As is often the case with corporate theatre, especially when you're springing surprises, the event started running late. Paul wanted a pee, but we couldn't leave the cupboard as he was in costume. And he couldn't take the costume off, in case we were called. So Paul crossed his legs and hung on (literally). Time dragged on. Still no cue.

You know how you want to pee more, when you know you can't go? We found a very large vase. I delicately turned my back while Paul availed himself of said vase. He was a happy actor. Eventually, we were summoned from our cupboard and the show went ahead. Darlings, we were a triumph! (Actor and script, that is.) It wasn't until we were celebrating in the pub afterwards, that we remembered... we never emptied the vase.

Conferences

Most large companies have conferences. These conferences serve a whole range of purposes, from acting as the company's AGM to using the opportunity of gathering the whole sales force or management in one room at one time to give them information.

They are usually day-long affairs and usually take place in huge auditoria such as the ICC in Birmingham, the Excel Centre in London, the SECC in Glasgow or other large venue, given that a full-scale sales conference can involve an audience of between 1,500 to 2,500 people. Sometimes, though less often these days, I think, in order to give everyone involved a quick holiday, these conferences are held in European capital cities.

The day might consist of an address from the CEO, and then various members of the executive team outlining current sales strategies and positions, with normally an exhortation to do that little bit better and a preview of what's coming up for them during the year ahead thrown in for good measure.

It's not unusual for a company to expect the audience to sit at one of these events for seven to eight hours a day. The clever production company planning this event for its client will try and lighten their load. High-energy music, video inserts and, quite often, clever use of acts from *Britain's Got Talent* will all enhance the experience for the participants.

Along with corporate role-play, this is the one sector of the corporate market in which I have had a great deal of personal experience. I have directed conferences for clients across the world. I have presented conferences. I have taken part in and directed comedy sketches used as linking material in conferences. I have used actors in a whole variety of roles in conferences.

You might be asked to take part in some scripted linking pieces for a major client. These pieces will most probably have been scripted especially for the event, and although the word 'comedy sketch' may have been used when you were booked for the job, you might now be scanning the script in a vain search for anything humorous. Do not be fooled. I have to say that one of the biggest laughs I have ever had in my career was when the actress Jan Goodman approached me on stage dressed in rags for me to utter the greeting:

> 'Ah, here comes the wife of a Canon executive who hasn't received his yearly bonus!'

On the other hand you can step onto the conference stage with a script that you think is rather funny and makes sense to you as an actor and receive absolutely no reaction whatsoever. You should remember that the audience sitting in front of you are not necessarily expecting a piece of theatre, comedy or not. They may already have engaged their brain into 'listen to senior director give dull financial presentation before getting drunk at company's expense this evening' mode. So you may play quite good material to very little reaction.

Whatever you're doing in the conference set-up, whether it be presenting or acting in linking material, you will be responsible to the producer.

A producer in the corporate world is the person who is organising the whole event for the production company on behalf of the client. There are some brilliant producers out there in the corporate market. Some have an awareness of what staging a piece of theatre entails, and a huge conference is a piece of theatre. Others have no theatrical awareness whatsoever and are simply good organisers. It is the producer who will be liaising with the client and the producer who has sorted out the deal with you via an agent (or not).

It is incredibly rare on a corporate event to find a 'director', as such. I tend to work as a creative director on conferences that I do, but this is mainly in relation to coaching the presentation delivery of the client. Most of the conferences I have performed in as a presenter or as an actor have never had a director running them. This does require you as an actor to keep your wits about you and to answer some questions such as 'Am I using the stage well?' for yourself.

You should realise that, in a conference situation, even as the main link presenter, you will not be the focus of everyone's attention. You will be expected to just get on with the job without any fuss. Indeed, most probably the only feedback you will receive until after the event will be about the things you're doing that they are *not* happy with.

The client is king and as such takes precedence at rehearsal. Some producers, who have what I call their 'think-ahead hats' on, may allow you to have a rehearsal as presenter before any client comes onto the site. Lots of producers, however, don't possess this piece of headgear. They will slot your linking pieces between more in-depth rehearsals for the client presentations and so you will hardly receive any attention whatsoever. That is unless, of course, you make a serious mistake. At this point the client will panic, run over to the producer and probably very loudly within earshot of yourself say: 'He's not going to be that terrible tomorrow, is he?'

Clients have no perception of what the rehearsal process is for. If they see you in rehearsal they expect you to be working at performance level. They expect to see what they have paid for.

After the conference is over, they will be full of praise for you, unless you really screwed it up. The praise for you, of course, brings an opportunity for you to praise them. To tell them how good they are, and how they should really be doing this professionally! You may find out more than you wish to about their dramatic aspirations, about how much they enjoy presenting, and about how they wish they had gone into it as a career rather than accountancy. Acknowledge it and try to keep a distance. No matter how enthused they are after the conference or show, no matter what promises they make, you can guarantee you will still have to fight for a place to present their next one. Corporate clients can appear to be very disloyal. It's not that they are, but it's just that many decisions taken in a large corporate organisation are made by a lot of people, and you can guarantee that, however good you were at this year's regional annual sales conference, they probably won't remember you when it comes to next year's.

Do the job. Do it well. Do it well all the time. Be prepared and be aware of what is needed from you.

One of the things you need to be aware of is whether your script will be on prompt or not.

Using Autocue

Prompt, or autocue, is a godsend if you're presenting a conference or acting in sketches that have lots of dialogue and technological information. It means that you don't have to learn the lines.

You do, however, have to be a reasonable sight-reader. No matter how much preparation you do, if working from autocue you will ultimately be reading. This is the talent that you need. Many very good actors are not good sight-readers. You should know your own ability in this field. If you feel you're not a good sight-reader, then using autocue is something you should certainly practise beforehand.

It is possible now to get an auto-prompt programme for your PC or Mac, your iPad or even your phone for less than £5, and in some instances for free. As with many skills, practice will make you perfect, or at least make you better. A little time invested here, and it's a new skill that you have to offer the corporate market.

In a conference situation, your script or dialogue will be displayed on a television monitor at the front of the stage, or on a screen at the back of the room. It may also be displayed on glass screens carefully placed so that you can see the scripts scrolling up on one side, but the audience see straight through the glass at you, the presenter or actor, from the other.

The main rule you should follow when autocue is present is to use it. Don't think: 'It will look much better if I learn it', because if you step onto the stage and start recalling your dialogue from memory at the same time as the words start rolling in front of you on monitors or glass screens, it won't be long before you lose your thread.

If autocue is present then spend time preparing your scripts so that you know what comes next and what you're talking about, but don't commit it to memory.

You shouldn't be tempted to rush. Just try to deliver the script as you would if it were conversation. Don't be afraid of pausing. Many people using autocue for the first time feel that they have to keep up with the machine. Don't worry. The autocue operators who work the conference circuit are incredibly experienced professionals. They have to be, as they have to support non-professional presenters of hugely varying ability. They cue the script to scroll at a pace they know is suitable for each speaker, and their patience and excellence in doing this is quite amazing. However, in a conference, they may have up to twenty-five scripts to cope with for a single day. This means there is a limited amount of work they can do on the layout of your script.

Ideally, you don't just want the words to scroll up on the screen. You want the words to be spaced so that you know how to deliver the presentation from how it looks on the screen.

Open up your script in a Word document. Speak it out loud to yourself and, each time you take a pause for sense or emphasis, break up the line in the document and start a new one.

You can then save this file as a Word document, or as a plain-text file, and either of these can be imported into the autocue system.

Below are two examples of script layout:

Here we see the script has just been copied in straight from a Word document as typed and has no layout for a speaker whatsoever. It would be difficult to present this text without giving the appearance of reading it.

Here the presenter has laid out the script so that how it appears on-screen is how they wish to speak it. This means that as you stand on the stage and the words are rolling up in front of you, you don't have to process the decisions you have made on delivery. They are laid bare in front of you in the layout of the text.

As with all staff at any conference, the autocue operator will be massively overworked. Have a quick discussion with them, and make them your friend. They are the person who is directly supporting you as you speak on the stage. Ask them if they mind you taking the script away to lay it out, and explain to them how you like it to work.

If you are working on a comedy sketch, which is just dialogue between two or more of you, and you don't want to use prompt, then make sure you agree with the producer that the monitor will display an empty black screen while you are doing the sketch. Personally speaking, as someone who finds it harder and harder to learn lots of lines as I get older, I'm always very grateful to know that prompt will be there.

In the world of the conference, where things can change at a moment's notice, the more support you can have in whatever form, the better.

Live Drama

A growing trend in the conference market is that of the specially created live drama. Particularly in the area of the medical conference, scripted plays highlighting the human issues of a condition are very much of the moment and, as such, are using quite a number of actors in the conference sector.

The play may have been commissioned by a marketing agency which represents a drug company. Medical conferences provide great opportunities for drug companies to meet, talk to, and focus on a large number of clinicians. The issues discussed at these conferences can quite often become cerebral and full of jargon and statistics. It can take a live drama to remind people that all these diseases and conditions affect human beings.

This is where actors come in. A well-written play lasting twenty to thirty minutes can create an effect that hours of lectures or promotional material can only strive for.

I've had the pleasure of directing several of these medical dramas. They can be quite lucrative and productive for the actors concerned. The first one I worked on, highlighting the issues around medicating young people with ADHD, was revived again and again for a period of two and a half years. It played at various medical conferences around the UK and provided regular work for its cast of five. On another occasion, a play for the world neurological conference took five actors and myself to Sydney for ten days for one performance. One of those rare and very pleasurable gigs that the corporate world can sometimes provide.

These plays are normally no longer than half an hour. Simply staged, with a minimum use of props, they will be rehearsed in as short a time as the production company can justify. You may find that luxuries such as technical and dress rehearsals are lacking, and that one quick runthrough on the stage at the venue is all that you're allowed. Again, this requires actors who are adaptable, and assured. You may have been asked to learn a large amount of material in a short time. If you are an actor who requires several days' work for your lines to sink in during rehearsal after you've learned them, then this sort of instant drama is probably not for you.

These projects are quite often priced as a package rather than on a daily rate. No one is going to pay five actors the daily rate that they would get as a conference presenter. The starting point for the production company in calculating the cost of these events will be: what would the actor expect to earn from a week's theatre work? I would suggest that a week of doing one of these dramas shouldn't be paid at less than around £750 per actor. I'm basing that on a figure of £500 for the rehearsals, and the extra work of line-learning, and the final figure of £250 for the performance day – based on one performance. All other performances would then be paid at the performance rate of £250. If you're offered less than these amounts for what is essentially a week's work, then you really should question how they are making up the fee.

Five out of the seven of these medi dramas that I have done have also been recorded onto DVD. In my case I'm lucky that I have a producer who is aware that this should represent an extra payment for the actors. They have been recorded in small green-screen studios, and the actors have also been paid for the recording day.

Many clients think that they will just be able to point a video camera at the play on the day at the conference and use the resulting footage for training purposes. You should ensure that any material recorded on the day is only as a record of the conference, and the play itself will not be used in any other way. Don't get bolshie about this. Ask at the time of booking, and double-check with the producer or director of the event, preferably when you're on-site.

The small dramas can bring the best of both worlds together. The joy of working with a small team of actors on a script that is emotion-based, and yet carefully cosseted by some of the luxuries of the corporate-conference world.

Interactive

There is one final area of live work that can sometimes be promotional, is often used at exhibitions and conferences and can sometimes venture into whole areas of its own. It has its roots in street theatre, and uses actors to create characters who can interact on various levels with members of the public. You'll often find these characters leading you into dinner on conference evening. They could be anything from paparazzi pressing for your photograph and pushing to interview you to oversize ringmasters, or egg-headed scientists interacting with you to solve some strange algebraic equation. They might be adorning a major stand at an international exhibition, or you could come across them in the street promoting an anti-litter campaign from a local authority.

This is character-based work taken to an extreme. Its purpose is to be eye-catching and involving. At its worst it can be putting on a bear suit and interacting with shoppers in a supermarket, but at its best it can be a chance to immerse yourself in a character for a few hours, mingle with the public and enjoy their reactions.

The Natural Theatre Company based in Bath are world leaders in this field, working in the areas of corporate entertainment, private parties and weddings, and also providing characters for public events and festivals – with the result that actors working with 'The Naturals' can find themselves doing a huge variety of jobs.

I spoke to the actress Daisy Douglas, who often works as an extremely accomplished street performer alongside her considerable theatre and television credits.

❝ I suppose I'm really lucky as working with the Natural Theatre Company has given me the opportunity to travel doing work I really enjoy. St Petersburg, Japan, Australia, Swindon... All over the world really.

Sometimes it's the most glorious thing you can do and sometimes it's not. Sometimes you're just not in a chatty, funny mood. The great thing about the way we work is that you are always part of the picture, part of the team. Some of the team will engage, and some can take a more passive role; and this can change throughout the time you're out doing the job. I never say 'yes' to jobs that I think are not going to make me feel good. For example, I have a problem doing things close to home or in areas where I think I might meet people I know. Sometimes the public being rude to you can affect you, and yet sometimes you can just turn it into a comedy gift.

I think it's really important to just be able to play the complete truth and understand the environment that you're working in. You might be in a town centre promoting something. People haven't come there to be entertained. They have come to shop, to meet people, to have coffee. To some of them you are an interesting and delightful addition to their day, but for others you could just be an unnecessary obstruction. Just because you're dressed up and having fun doesn't mean that everyone else is.

I think more than anything you have to be really sure that you're not going to be embarrassed about it.

A Final Word on Live Events

And in a way Daisy's final piece of advice is useful for anybody thinking of working in the live-events market. Think of that play you might have been in where you began to doubt that the script was really as good as you thought it was. Think of that show you were in that didn't get the reactions you'd hoped for and made you begin to doubt its worth. Then multiply that by at least five hundred times, and that's the sort of feeling you will get doing live-events work that you're embarrassed about. Interacting with the public at close range, and not being really sure that you like what you're doing, is a little like doing children's theatre to an unbelieving audience of six-year-olds. Very very quickly they'll let you know what they think of you… and it won't be nice!

If the brief doesn't excite you and you're not sure you'll like it, then it's probably best to stay away from it. I'm hoping there has been something you have read about in this chapter that has made you think: 'Yes, brilliant, I'd really love to give that a go.' If so, that's great. Go for it. Make those events part of the target of your business plan which we're going to take a look at in Chapter 9. If you have any doubts, then stay clear.

You're not the only person who might have doubts about aspects of the corporate market. Sometimes people don't understand it at all. They don't appreciate what it is currently doing and what opportunities it can provide, and at worst they think it's just an unnecessary diversion to tempt actors away from their true vocation.

In the next chapter, we'll find out who those people might be and what they really do think…

To Tweet or Not to Tweet

For many of us, social media are an integral part of our daily lives. However we display our presence on web, we like to fill our quiet moments with comments and status updates. Witty appraisals showing our state of mind to our friends and acquaintances.

Beware!

You wouldn't be the first person to have been caught out by an indiscreet tweet or Facebook status regarding their work. As I was writing this, a contestant on the ITV reality talent show *Superstar* incurred the wrath of Lord Lloyd Webber himself by tweeting his picture with a crown of thorns. An indiscreet claim on the role of winner.

There will be lots of moments when you have downtime on a corporate gig. You'll be sitting around kicking your heels while clients rehearse, or you will be waiting for other role-plays to finish. These are dangerous moments. Hands stray towards the smartphone and a virtual indiscretion can be committed quite quickly.

I have actually seen on a Twitter feed: 'boring afternoon's role-play for International Holdings. Jerks for managers. #losingthewilltolive'. On this occasion, the actor concerned was lucky. He hadn't tagged the client correctly on Twitter, and his tweet wasn't picked up. The big corporate firms have remote Twitter scanners, or Twitbots as I believe they're called, that scan the network for any mention of their name. If you don't believe me, just enter Marks & Spencer into a tweet and see how quickly you get a response.

The work you are doing is professional. It is also confidential. You should not be commenting on it. The best advice I was given about Twitter was not to tweet anything that you would not stand at your front door and shout. It is good advice, and when you're away doing a corporate job you're nowhere near your front door, so don't shout!

Even an innocent comment like: 'had a brilliant afternoon doing role-play training for International Holdings' can be unwelcome as that particular company may not want people to know they are training people. The golden rule here is that, unless you have expressly been told otherwise, you don't comment on your corporate work on social media.

There will be very rare occasions when a client will ask you to do otherwise. Clients who are arranging high-profile entertainment events with big names may want to boast about this and may actively seek a presence in the virtual world for their event. That's fine, but double-check with the client as to what content you should be putting up and if possible let them provide the comment.

It's so easy to get caught out so don't give yourself the opportunity. And, of course, stay away from your phone or BlackBerry while you're doing the job. There's nothing more infuriating for a client than to see people whose attention is not entirely on what they're being paid for.

8

Agents, Equity…
And Attitudes

I'm sure it's clear to you by now that the corporate world is a varied marketplace in which actors can thrive by using use their specific skills.

Although recent years and the current recession have seen a cutback in both events and training, companies still have budgets to spend. It is a foolish company that cuts back severely on training in a recession. They may well find themselves with a workforce who are unequipped for the next period of growth, so, while the opportunities may have diminished in number since the economic downturn of 2008, both the variety of work and the opportunity for actors to diversify continues unabated.

Attitudes to this marketplace can be confusing. Some people hardly know of its existence.

While I was writing this book, I had agreed to deliver a couple of one-day courses on role-play skills at The Actors Centre. These classes have proved popular in the past. Indeed, any class which looks like it might lead to work for an actor proves popular.

It was therefore interesting to see one morning on Twitter that The Actors Centre had tweeted 'Corporate work isn't the most glamorous, but it can pay the bills'.

I can guarantee that the person who tweeted that is now hanging by his ankles over a crocodile-infested foot spa, but at the same time it's easy to understand why this perception exists. Yet corporate work can put you in some of the nicest hotels you will have stayed in. It can take you all over Europe, if not the world. It's true that, as you step onto the aircraft, you are unlikely to be seated in first class, but it's not unknown.

Sometimes these luxuries are available only for the shortest period. I once took a cast of eight actors down to Bournemouth where we were staging a musical for the launch of Nutri-Grain, the Kellogg's breakfast-cereal bar. Having rehearsed in the venue all day, on a stage with two revolves, back projection and with a sound system the like of which most rep theatres would kill for, the actors and I crossed the road to the hotel in which we were staying the night.

After checking in, there was a lot of hurrying along corridors followed by the sound of actorly screams of delight, as the cast discovered their rooms were balconied suites with hot tubs and sauna cabins. One particularly lucky actor found himself in the penthouse suite with a stunning view from his three glass walls!

Sadly, the time to enjoy all this hospitality was minimal. We were being taken out by the client for a Chinese meal at eight o'clock, from which we returned a little merrier at nearly midnight. Our call for a runthrough the next day was for nine in the morning, and so the opportunity to use all the complimentary toiletries was limited. But I do seem to remember that the actor who had drawn the lucky straw and got the penthouse had to host a couple of games of Team Charades before anyone was ready to go to bed. Also, our stay there provided me with one of my great learning points from the corporate world: hotel shower caps make great salad covers. Bring them home and save on cling film!!

Sometimes a corporate event can bring you stunning food and great catering. Sometimes you can be shoved in a back room with a plate of lukewarm chilli and a salad that is positively crawling towards the door.

You might find that it is actually up to you to deal with the situation when things are not going right. Most other jobs that you have done will have been organised by your agent and will have had the protection of Equity in the form of a contract or agreement. As the corporate opportunities available to actors diversify, so the role of the actor's agent and of Equity have changed.

Agents

There was a time, only about five or six years ago, when I would call an agent to do an availability check on an actor for a corporate job, to find that my call was not returned. On some occasions, I would then speak to the actor directly, only to hear that they had never been told of my enquiry. Some agents have been known not to consider corporate work at all. But things do seem to have changed recently.

These days agents do have to take the corporate world more seriously. In times when a day's role-play can bring you a fee slightly more than an episode of *Doctors*, agents have to think outside the box if they want to keep their clients busy.

But how, when it comes to corporate work, do you manage that relationship with your agent?

In my survey, 97 per cent of actors questioned said that they had done some form of corporate work, but only 17 per cent said that this work had come through their agent.

Do you pay commission on it?

Only 10 per cent of those actors who had done corporate work said that they paid commission on the work to their agent, whether it had come through their agent or not. 44 per cent said they paid commission if the agents got them the work, and 46 per cent said they never paid commission to their agents on corporate work.

Yet each day you are out doing corporate work, role-playing, or working on a job that you have got for yourself, is a day that your agent can't use you, a day that you can't be earning commission for them.

And how does your agent feel about the fact that you might not be available for work that they are putting you up for? In the fifteen years that I've been with my current agent, there has mercifully been only one occasion where some filming dates on a job that she had got me clashed with a corporate that I had already booked myself. You will find it takes a lot of work to maintain a relationship with your agent to ensure this doesn't happen more often.

The main rule here is to keep your agent informed. Let them know as soon as possible about corporate jobs you have accepted which will make you unavailable for jobs they have suggested you for. Just how many times a year you can do this before your agent despairs of you will vary from agent to agent, so talk it through with them. Let them know how serious you are about your corporate work and what it means to you – financially and in terms of being out there working.

63 per cent of the agents who answered my survey said that they would respond to corporate enquiries that came into the office specifically: i.e. as a result of a phone call or direct email from the corporate casting director. Only 31 per cent said that they actively chased corporate jobs sent out on casting briefs – services such as Castweb and Spotlight, and sent to all agents as a round-robin newsletter. The remaining 6 per cent openly admitted that they would prefer actors to be available for television and film work so the corporate world was looked on as a last resort.

89 per cent of responding agents said they did have clients who do role-play work, with 73 per cent of agents saying that they only took commission on that work if they had secured it for the actor. 21 per cent of agents, however, did

say that they took commission on such work even if the actors had sourced the work themselves, as they regarded such work as getting in the way of possible jobs that they might be putting their client up for.

One of the major problems that agents encounter is that actors acquire role-play or corporate work themselves and then don't tell their agent. When the agent calls with an interview for the day in question, the actor is already committed to a piece of work on which the agent will not be earning commission. The agent's reputation with their contacts such as directors and casting directors is then also called into question. Nearly 53 per cent of the agents in the survey said that they had encountered problems with clients in this sort of area. Many agents would expect that clients who were committed to role-play jobs should be able to get out of them by having a cover of some sort if a better opportunity, e.g. an interview, arose.

17 per cent of the agents surveyed said that they would price an actor higher for a corporate enquiry than they would for an enquiry for more mainstream work. Agents who do so are really out of touch with what is happening in the corporate world these days. Gone are the days when the very word 'corporate' had actors dreaming of a holiday for themselves and their family in the Maldives. The corporate companies have grown wise as to what they should be paying, and while they might still be happy to pay the price of a detached house to a 'television face' for a major corporate campaign, in general they have learnt that there is always an actor available to do the job they want at the price they want to pay.

Several of the agents who responded to the survey said that a major problem with corporate work is that money is the only reward. No one is going to see you perform with a view to casting you in theatre, film or television, so it's very limiting. The agents felt that the payments on these sorts of jobs really should reflect this as much as possible. However, agents did in general agree that it was much better to be working on some kind of performing rather than 'stocking the shelves of a supermarket'. As one agent put it: 'Acting is a business and it is better for any actor to be earning money rather than resting and waiting for that dream job.'

Equity

Equity, the actor's union, plays a vital part in the lives of all actors. If you are of my generation then an Equity card was a golden ticket. The closed-shop union system that existed in those days meant that you couldn't get work as an actor without an Equity card – and you couldn't get an Equity card unless you could prove you had worked as an actor. If you couldn't get a repertory-theatre job which had an Equity card with it, then you probably did a series of dubious variety acts in pubs and old people's homes to get a set of contracts in the hope that Equity wouldn't look at them too closely and would offer you a card.

I'm sure my relationship with Equity is similar to that of most actors. I bemoan the fact that I have to fork out my subscription each year, and yet I'm grateful that it is there to help out when needed. You get the benefit of Equity having negotiated a minimum salary level. And you do have somebody on the other end of the phone just to talk to even if they can't help. I would absolutely recommend to any young person starting out that they should join Equity.

But what of Equity and the corporate world? Does it have any influence? Can it offer any protection to its members working in the corporate market?

Most of my corporate work has not been done under the auspices of Equity. In fact, I don't think I have ever signed an Equity contract for anything that I would deem to be a corporate job. It's not deliberate practice, it's just that they don't seem to exist or to be around.

For live corporate events it might be possible that the standard Equity variety contract could be used. In practice, most corporate agents, if offering a contract at all, will offer one of their own. Many bookings are just done by a confirmation email and an assumption that you will invoice them once the job is done.

Role-play, which is the corporate sector that affects most actors, does fall under the auspices of an Equity agreement. A role-play agreement was produced in 2003 and was based on a contract used by one particular major role-play company. It was drawn up in response to a motion that requested Equity produce minimum guidelines. Equity say that this was never circulated to role-play companies, but only sent out to members for them to use as a benchmark. The reasoning behind this was specifically to ensure that higher rates or better terms of the agreement were not discouraged.

This would seem to have two flaws. Although it wasn't circulated, or, to quote Equity, 'promulgated', to the role-play companies, they did, of course, learn of its existence. They became aware of the figures in the agreement. At that time the going rate for a day's role-play was around £200 a day, with many people earning more than that. On the publication of the Equity agreement, many companies were able to drop their daily rate to the £175 listed in the agreement as the minimum acceptable.

Although Equity will deny it, it's a common occurrence throughout the profession in all its branches that the Equity minimum becomes the agreed wage. This is what happened in role-play, as the Equity agreement leaked out to the role-play companies.

They weren't told to use it. After all, Equity had not 'promulgated' it to them. It seemed that Equity was placing the responsibility on its own members. You would be offered a job and you would be expected to offer up a contract, or to specify that you wanted an Equity contract sending. This was never going to work.

Equity does not seem to be sure of how to deal with role-play and actors who do it. This agreement was last updated in 2007.

It's always going to be incredibly difficult for Equity to have any real effect in this market. The corporate role-play sector is, after all, a free market. It has no trade associations to bind the various companies together and represent them. Therefore it's not possible for Equity to have a collective dialogue with these companies and ensure standard terms and dispute procedures. Equity is incredibly limited as to what it can do here.

It has talked to the major role-play providers, but the lack of a trade association with whom the union can negotiate means that these companies involved will be anxious not to be seen to attempt to operate as an illegal cartel, and Equity can't be put in the position of being seen to create one.

Perhaps what Equity needs to do is come up with a series of guidelines. A code of practice. For example, they could agree that the expenses part of any role-play contract will be paid within seven days of the job on production of an invoice. Quite often as a role-play actor you will incur expenses of up to £100 or so (more if flying) on travel and taxis. You will invoice this along with your fee. Sometimes it has been known for the role-play companies not to pay an invoice for up to sixty days. Many of the smaller ones simply do not have the cash-flow, and they are reliant on their client paying them before they can pay the actors. This means that if you do three or four jobs a month you could be three or four hundred pounds out of pocket waiting to be reimbursed. An Equity code of recommendation could change this.

Although the existing agreement has some guidelines as to working times, no maximum session time is in place, only a maximum working day.

There are good things in the existing contract. A cancellation scheme, and the 'confirmation of dates' clause which agrees when a date is a firm booking, but there are many other things that could be included or modified. These could be put into an Equity code of agreed practice. This could be given a logo or Kitemark, and role-play companies could choose to sign up to it. Actors would then know that they are dealing with a company which is prepared to work in a certain way. Each job would continue to be negotiated depending on market rates, competition and number of actors, but agreed standards would be in place re: working hours, conduct, expenses, etc.

Equity told me that they would 'most probably' help members wherever they can, if, for example, they are not paid for role-play work. But that:

> Equity has to devote as a priority its fairly thin
> resources to deliver members good agreements in the
> organised sector of live and recorded media, together
> with the various individual disputes and problems
> that arise from members working on these contracts
> and agreements. This is the union's core work, and it
> is of primary importance to members.

However, when it comes to assessing income to determine the level of subscription, Equity isn't so backward!

My feeling is that only monies earned on Equity contracts should be used in assessing income for subscription purposes.

If Equity is actually going to involve itself in the corporate role-play market then it needs to do so clearly, openly and effectively.

Until Equity involves itself in the corporate role-play market, I suggest it might be best to not consider monies from role-play as part of your earnings.

In response to my various queries and after the interviews at the Equity office, I was promised 'a quote for my book' from Christine Payne, the General Secretary:

66 Equity understands that our members are employed by a number of corporate employers to exercise their acting skills in role-play work. Some of our members have successfully supported themselves in the profession by obtaining such work and using their skills in this way. Equity provides the usual raft of services to its members when they undertake role-play work including legal, insurance and general advice. Given the disparate nature of this industry Equity is keen to set down guidelines to mutually benefit both our members and the various employers to ensure consistent and decent standards covering role-play work.

Which basically seems to say that 'We know it's out there, though we are not really sure what to do about it.'

It would be great if Equity could put something in place. I understand they are sending out a survey to members. Hopefully this will reveal to them what they seem not to know: that there are a huge number of actors working out there in the corporate market, many of whom make their living solely from that source. If Equity wants to have this work counted as part of an actor's income, then Equity needs to take action. Do something concrete, something effective, and something of benefit to both sides. Let's hope this happens soon.

Casting Directors

In the world of acting that you are already familiar with, i.e. that of the stage and screen, the casting director is god. These are the people who can make sure that you get in front of a director for a job. They are also the people who can decide that you're *not* the person who should be seen or given an interview. It's frustrating when that happens, but for the director, casting directors are a vital filter, a conduit to ensure that the valuable time slots of the casting day are filled with people who are suited to the role.

You and I as actors are often not as objective as we should be about our suitability. As a young actor I would go into most interviews thinking: 'What do you want me to be? I'm an actor. I can be it.' Now as an older actor I'm more of the mindset: 'This is what I am. Do you want it?' It's not a case of having closed down my options or accepted the pressures of typecasting. It's just knowing more about what I'm suited to and what I'm best at.

In all areas, casting directors develop a pool of actors that they know well. Most casting directors are very good about getting out to see theatre and becoming familiar with actors' work. And so the director can trust the person doing the casting to put three or four very suitable choices in front of him for each role.

In the world of corporate work, quite often, companies won't use a casting director as quite simply they don't want to pay the cost. Many of them don't really understand the function of the casting director and are quite happy to give the job to somebody in their office. This means putting out a casting brief on one of the online casting services and receiving a huge number of CVs submitted from actors and agents alike. In this instance, I think they tend to work mainly from the photograph. There is no knowing if the person at the corporate production company has any breadth of knowledge regarding television and theatre credits, and it may be just down to their personal likes or dislikes. Your submission really does need to focus on your relevance to the job.

I've been casting corporate videos and live events since around 1996. Having been used as an actor myself by a lot of production companies, I established myself as having a reputation for knowing what the best kind of actors were for corporate jobs. Production companies then began to ring me: 'We don't have anything for you on this job, but we wondered if you could find us a couple of young guys who would be suitable?' So began what has been an intermittent career as a corporate casting director.

I, too, always begin by looking through the people I know. People I have worked with. Corporate events can often make tricky demands on actors, and it's not only their talent that is assessed, but also their temperament, their suitability.

If I am not able to cast a 'corporate' from the pool of actors I've already worked with, then I will put the casting brief out to certain agents that I know or trust. Many actors would be surprised about the manner in which their CVs are sometimes submitted by agents. I've had submissions for jobs consisting of a one-line email saying: 'Please find our suggestions attached.' This doesn't help. It is then left to me to wade through masses of CVs, with no help or guiding comments from the agent.

The best agents are the people who will include a short note with the submission as to why they believe that actor is suitable for the brief. They'll point out similar work that they may have done in the past. It's an incredible help.

Similarly, actors will sometimes submit themselves for the jobs, particularly if I have put out the brief on one of the casting services that are currently available.

Out of choice I would always use Castweb – www.castweb.co.uk. I know the people running it, and I know they issue guidelines to the actors who subscribe to it about how carefully they should think before submitting themselves for jobs that are listed. Actors, however, are not the most objective judges of what they are suitable for. It's not unknown to get an email from an actor, and I quote here, that says (sic):

```
Please consider me for your job as I
would be gud fer it.
```

A good casting letter can make a great impression. Remember, many people casting corporate work don't cast for a living, but what they may do very often is conduct job interviews. That's the key to getting an interview.

A well-laid-out letter. State who you are and why you're writing.

Dear Stephen,

My name is Paul Clayton and I'd like to take this opportunity to apply for the role of the Microsoft Conference presenter which I know you're currently casting.

Follow this with no more than three reasons as to why you consider yourself suitable. If this is previous experience (i.e. you've done a similar job before), then you can highlight that job on your attached CV. If it's a skill that is making you suitable (i.e. fluency in a foreign language), then a small amount of information as to where you acquired that can also help.

Make sure you end the letter with your objective. The objective is a meeting. Don't be afraid of asking for this.

It would be really great to get the opportunity to meet with you, and I hope this is something we can arrange. I look forward to hearing from you...

The attitude that this is a job interview should be carried through to the meeting itself. Unless you know you're going up for a particular role in a drama-based project, dress smartly. These days job interviews in many fields no longer demand a suit, shirt and tie, but dress well and look good. Remember, you can always take the tie off when you get there if you feel overdressed, but you can't put it on if haven't got it with you in the first place.

The person you're meeting with may not be used to working with actors, so try and keep your answers as concise as possible. They want to feel confident in the fact that you can do the job. Good eye contact, good listening skills, and some well-prepared questions, can all help you convey this. Quite often at the interview stage of a corporate job, the client hasn't fully decided what they're looking for. The meeting is your opportunity to show them what is possible. If it's a live event, you could be working with the client and the production company for several days of very long hours. This interview is a chance for them to see how they might get on with you.

I'm not naive enough to think that everyone reading this book will immediately give up everything they've been doing so far and launch themselves headlong into the corporate world. I know many actors will want to extend their work opportunities by adding corporate work.

But is there a stigma attached to corporate jobs and the actors who do them?

Since I don't myself cast any mainstream television, film or theatre, I was very interested to find out what casting directors who do work in those spheres felt about the corporate market. Especially as, in the survey I undertook as part of my preparation in writing this book, 75 per cent of actors surveyed said that they thought casting directors looked down on corporate work.

I talked to four casting directors who I respect, and who (by no mean coincidence) have all cast me in various television or theatre jobs. Two of the four had cast corporate videos, training videos or internet projects.

You may be very proud of a corporate video project that you have taken part in, but is it worth listing it on your CV for other work?

One casting director I spoke to said:

❝ I have come across directors and producers (particularly in drama) who are very 'sniffy' about such credits. There can be a perception that it's the sort of work that is only undertaken by actors of low ability. I think that attitude is changing, particularly amongst the younger directors and producers, but it can still be an issue. I would suggest that actors don't put a disproportionate number of corporate credits on their CVs. I would say the same about commercial credits too.

If the casting director doesn't already know you, it can be quite hard for them to judge the type of role you might be suitable for as they might not be familiar with the demands of the role of Second Transit Van Driver in 'A Ford you can afford!'

The casting directors were unanimous in the feeling that actors should 'go for it' on this sort of work, but be careful about alluding to it too much when going for non-corporate work. Be aware that there are misguided perceptions about the whole corporate and commercial world out there. Tailor your interview technique to the job you're going for.

If you are being cast for a corporate or commercial, then it's a positive benefit to talk about similar work you've done in the past. If you are being seen for a television/film/theatre/drama project, it's probably better to stress the drama roles you've undertaken in the past. In these days of the 'cut and paste' CV there really is no excuse for you not to have CVs that are tailored to each area of work.

Make sure you know, and have in the contract, exactly what the work is being used for. If they say it's exclusively for an intranet (i.e. a corporate website video) and then it ends up on YouTube, it might not be a performance or quality of work that you would want to go public or that you would want a casting director to find when they are looking for a sample of your work.

You should try to find out when submitting yourself for a corporate brief whether the casting director is someone working for the production company, or a casting director who is used to having a wider brief. If it's the former, then you should focus on corporate work that you've done, but it would do no harm to include any notable television credits you have. It's hardly likely that someone working in an event company based in Fulham will have seen your *Hedda Gabler* at Dundee Rep, but they may be intrigued by the fact that you played 'Third Fashionista' in the recent Christmas special of *Absolutely Fabulous*. Never underestimate the power of television.

Remember, here you are submitting a casting suggestion that has to sell you. It is what people understand in the corporate market.

The main thing for you to bear in mind is that casting directors are also trying to make their reputation too. It's hardly likely that they're going to do it by casting a viral video for the NHS.

Tailor your cut to your cloth, as they say. Your corporate work will hopefully become a vital part of your working life, a source of income, and something that can give you a sense of fulfilment. It's not likely to increase your employability in more mainstream sectors of the industry.

Ultimately, what casting directors are very good at is matching people to jobs that they are suitable for. They may not push the boundaries as often as we would like. It is possible that their choices may sometimes be thought of as dull, but they are excellent in putting the right people in front of the appropriate directors or producers, whether it is a major movie, or a promotional campaign for a shampoo.

What's on your CV is what they will use to determine your suitability, so in the end the answer is in your own hands. You can create the right CV for the right job, the right conversation in the right interview.

And that stands for getting the work too!

Summary

Getting cast when the corporate is being cast by a recognised casting director:

1. Clear CV.

2. Be honest as to your abilities.

3. Make sure your corporate credits are prominent on the CV.

4. Include other good credits that show your versatility and status as an actor.

Getting cast when the corporate is being cast by someone from the company:

1. Change your CV so that your corporate credits are prominent and the rest of your work is very selective.

2. Make sure the CV is accompanied by a covering letter which focuses on your suitability for the job.

3. Find out as much as you can about the client (the company the job is for) before the interview.

4. Dress smartly. It's a job interview.

❝ In the spring of 1997, I was asked to perform in a corporate event for an international fast-food chain at the ICC in Birmingham. We performed sketches and game-show pastiches filled with the company's in-jokes and jargon, and included an award ceremony for outstanding employees. This all built to a climax of signed footballs being kicked out into the audience by professional footballers.

The director had asked me to take part because he knew I was a football fanatic and played for an amateur team. He needed an actor with 'ball skills' (was the term he used, I seem to remember). His knowledge of the game was poor so when he told me that Dwight Yorke, David Platt and David Beckham were the stars involved, he was amused and slightly bewildered by my excitement. He said each actor would take responsibility for looking after one particular footballer.

'Which one would you like to look after?' he asked.

'David Beckham,' I replied. No hesitation.

David Beckham was my hero. I was going to kick a ball to my hero!!!

When the day arrived I was incredibly excited and when Beckham walked into the green room to be introduced, I found that I had lost the power of speech. I shook his hand, trying desperately to seem cool and professional and mumbled something unintelligible whilst fighting the urge to curtsey.

After about half an hour I started to relax a little and ran through with him all the details and staging of the event. Then I started to chat. 'So, David,' I asked, 'What's it like as a Londoner being up in Manchester? Do people give you any stick for being a southerner?'

'Actually,' I continued, 'that's a really stupid question to ask you isn't it, I mean wherever you are you probably going to be treated like some sort of deity, aren't you?' He looked at me very strangely and asked 'Some sort of what?' I remember smiling at him and saying, 'It doesn't matter.'

The event went without a hitch. I didn't buckle under the pressure when my moment came. I managed to make every shot land perfectly for him, not bad when you think how large the stage at the ICC is.

Just before they left, I asked to have a photo taken with him, having sneaked in a camera. I wanted to capture this moment.

I have that photo on my mantelpiece to this day. Looking at it right this minute I notice that my smile is as wide as the Grand Canyon. A memory of a wonderful job that will stay with me for ever.

Andy Spiegel

9

Work…

And How to Get It

So you now understand the principles of role-play. You have looked through all the different possibilities available to you in the live event market. You are beginning to think what your special skills might be most suited for. The big question remains: how do you get the work?

On many occasions throughout this book you will be aware that I have referred to the fact that this is a business sector. It's not arty, it's not fluffy, and sometimes it's not caring. It's a business sector and it is looking for a commodity, a specially honed skill, or a service. The important word is business.

You may be one of those actors who are very good about running their career as a business.

At drama school I was privileged enough to have a lovely old tutor called John Macgregor. Every Friday morning for two hours he taught us all those fantastic bits of acting technique such as the double-take, the slow-burn, how to answer a telephone, and how to make a sip of a drink in an Agatha Christie to heighten the tension. He had started out as a promising young hopeful during the 1950s and indeed played alongside Olivier at Stratford. Stardom hadn't beckoned, but he had worked for over three decades as a jobbing actor, making a living out of it. He was full of brilliant advice as to how you actually managed the job of acting.

The two pearls of wisdom that I remember and indeed have tried to adhere to are:

- Do one thing each day that might lead to work and then get on with living your life.

- Do your accounts every Sunday.

Both of these have helped me develop what I hope has been a businesslike attitude to my career. You are allowed to do more than one thing each day to get work, but the principle behind his advice was that if you spend the whole day bemoaning the fact that you are out of work as an actor, you forget to live as a person. Soon you will be taking the shell of that person into each interview.

And as for the second piece of advice, every Sunday morning when I'm at home, listening to the delights of *I'm Sorry I Haven't A Clue* or *Just a Minute* just before brunch, you will find me doing my invoicing and accounts.

You're going to need a sense of discipline and organisation in order to make a success of yourself in the corporate world. Above all, you're going to need a plan.

Making Your Plan for Work

You are moving into a world where business plans are made daily. Objectives are set and markers are put into place so that the achievement of these objectives can be clearly judged. These are the techniques that you should begin to employ as you develop your plan to acquire corporate work and move into the corporate sector.

Create a document. Most likely you're going to do this on your computer, but there's nothing wrong with taking a large blank sheet of paper and physically writing down how this plan will be laid out.

You need to decide what the specific areas are that you feel you might be suited for within the corporate world. Hopefully from reading this book you have hit upon something that you feel is appropriate for you. Something in the

live-event field may have caught your eye. The idea of offering training may be appealing to you. You may have been
attracted by the skills involved in role-play. Whatever it is,
write down your target at the top of that document.

There is a school of thought, of course, that if you set up a
lot of targets and fire a lot of arrows, you're bound to hit one.
This is not necessarily the case. A focused, properly
researched campaign is the strategy that is most likely to
move you forward and help you achieve your goal.

Perhaps you might list the qualities you feel you have and
then align these qualities with the various areas of the corporate world that we have talked about.

For example, if comedy improvisation is your forte, then
perhaps the world of live events or murder-mystery
evenings is something that you would be well suited to.
Training sessions for the student doctor on how to break
bad news might be something you should avoid!

Once you've decided the area you're going to target, open
your browser, and enter into your search engine criteria that
will give you some possible contacts.

In the appendices of this book I have listed the companies I
have talked about in the text, but there are so many more.
The Spotlight guide *Contacts* has a page of role-play companies. Just entering 'live event production companies UK'
into Google instantly brought me up several pages of companies who create the sort of events that use actors.

This can become your database.

The next step, of course, is to make a targeted approach.
How many of these companies actually do use actors who
they have not met or do not know?

The solution is to find out. Read what the company has to
say about itself. Look at the events they have created. They
will be displaying some of their client list and past events on

their site in order to attract new business. How many of these events look as though they have used actors? Perhaps do a cross search and check on the website of the client to see whether there is a report on the success of the event.

Most of these live-event companies' websites will have a 'Contact Us' button. Click on it and see what it brings up. Most probably it will give you a form, which you would fill in if you were making an enquiry as to staging an event. The email addresses of key personnel at the company may also be listed. Look for the email addresses of the producers.

At this point you might be tempted to attach a letter to your CV and photograph as if you are applying for a theatre job. The difference here, of course, is that you cannot be absolutely sure how these companies get their actors. They may only use actors who come on personal recommendation. They may occasionally hold open castings.

The first stage is for you to email them and find out. Be open, honest and brief! Don't send a long email at this point listing the fact that five years ago you were a fire chief in *Emmerdale* and recently you played Henry IV in an open-air production at a coastal castle. Unless the email is reaching the person who understands what actors do, this would render the CV worthless. As in the days when actors spent whole afternoons writing twenty or thirty letters to repertory companies looking for work and received possibly one reply if they were lucky, so your email trawl through these companies may elicit few responses.

The company may respond by telling you that they do use actors, but only on an event-by-event basis. The good news is that you now have a contact at the company to whom you could reply and enquire when would be the best time to send in a CV and photograph. You might even enquire whether it would be possible to come in and say hello. The important thing here is to try and begin a dialogue with someone.

Emails are even easier to delete than CVs and photographs are to tear up and bin! It is always a sight that has saddened me as a theatre director to watch lots of actors' ten-by-eight photographs, for which they have paid from their own pocket, being torn up by theatre staff and put into the waste. Yet these photographs were not ones that were sent in response to a specific casting brief. They were the photographs that were sent unsolicited, asking to be kept on file for whenever something 'appropriate' came up. Theatres never really had the staff or the space to manage such a backlog of information.

It is certainly easier now in the age of electronic information, but the key to making sure that your CV is actually looked at is to get it into somebody's inbox at the moment when they are thinking about an event.

It is my privilege to know a huge number of very talented and fun-to-work-with actors. Even though my starting point for casting any corporate event is my folder of actors I have previously worked with, some escape my memory every time. It can be a chance meeting, the viewing of an old television programme, or a conversation that can put them back in my mind for a project.

What you must aim to do is to distinguish yourself from the large number of actors who send a generic mail-out to a huge number of production companies.

This is going to take time. Of course it is. You may spend a full afternoon and at the end of it have only sent off ten emails to the people you have managed to target. But if these are ten properly targeted emails to people in companies who have the relevant responsibility, then your chances of success are already higher.

Exactly the same approach applies to the role-play companies. All of the leading role-play training companies get a large number of generic applications from actors every day. Letters as emails saying:

```
Dear Role-play Company,

As a talented actor with a large number
of credits I'm currently looking to
expand my work opportunities into the
role-play industry. Please would you
contact me if anything suitable comes
up.
```

Of course, the astute account manager at the role-play company opens the letter or email and reads:

```
Dear Role-play Company,

As an actor who is currently out of
work and desperate, I'm trying to pick
up something from role-play, as I know
some actors do this. Please give me a
job.
```

You should target the role-play companies in exactly the same way that you target the live-event companies. Do a web search. Read up about the company. Find out what their strengths are. Look at the names of the account managers. Who are their clients? Do you know any actors who have worked with them and might recommend you? Use the links on the website to contact them and enquire how they recruit their actors.

You may get a response saying that they have an awful lot of actors on their books at the moment and don't have enough work for them. This will very probably be the case with many of the companies. However, the good thing about this is that they are actors. Actors who, alongside their role-play work, are still doing film and television work and therefore rendering themselves unavailable for jobs in the corporate market. Every role-play company has a shifting workforce. Sometimes they get larger jobs which require specific skills, and it's at this point that you, the new role-player, can be immensely useful to them.

Ask them how they like actors to approach them. Then, whatever they say, that should guide your approach. If they do reply saying that they already have an enormous number of actors, respond to them and say thank you for getting back in touch and when would be a good time for you to mail them again?

Don't then delete them from your list. Start a new list of contacts and dates. Make a note of when they suggested that you might get in touch, and be sure to follow it up at that point.

Again, establish a dialogue with somebody at the company. Try and verify that this is someone who ultimately does make decisions regarding actors, but treat them with respect.

It's always interesting as to where feedback on actors comes from. Many are the casting days I have done on the theatre productions that I have directed where a friend of mine, or a friendly ASM, has managed the waiting auditionees and ushered them into the room. At the end of the day, feedback as to how the actors behaved while they were waiting and chatting to their peers is invaluable. On more than one occasion someone's behaviour outside an audition room has taken them out of the running for a job.

So, from that very first email, treat the person as though they are a decision maker. They might only be a gatekeeper, but, like the dreaded doctor's receptionist, you're not going to get an appointment without their help.

The Letter and CV

You have very probably written letters for work before. Few actors haven't. There may be a lucky number who have always relied on their agent to get the work for them and have been successful, but the majority of actors will at some point or other have penned a letter themselves asking for a job.

The theatre world tends to be more forgiving about application letters from actors than perhaps it should be. In the past when putting out casting calls on Castweb, I have received letters in all forms, from the heavily formatted and highly ornate personalised-stationery letter to the one scrawled on a sheet torn out of a lined notebook.

These days, turning out well-formatted business letters is a piece of cake using any of the popular word-processing programmes on home computers. Again, you have to play the business world at their own game.

A clear, well-laid-out and brief covering letter which explains why you're writing should accompany the CV. Ideally, the letter should have a clear objective. You may be asking for an audition. You may be asking to come into the office for a chat. A letter that asks something is more likely to produce a response.

Some companies may request submissions by email alone. You should be careful that the email is not too informal. Email is a medium used for everything from a friendly conversation to full-scale business requests. Make sure the tone and layout of your email are appropriate. You are writing to a company who are assessing your ability to work in a business environment. Your letter or email will be the first opportunity they have to do this.

Just as the computer helps us to turn out high-quality application letters with ease, so it allows us to produce CVs pertinent to a particular job. As I have already said, in these days of 'cut and paste', there really is no excuse for sending out one generic CV listing all your credits for every job. A CV for a television role should list your television credits first and foremost, probably then backed up by your theatre credits. Vice versa if you're applying to the National, the RSC, or a rep.

Skills from other jobs that you may have thought would be of no use to you as an actor can sometimes be positive assets to put on an application to a role-play company. If you have been a teacher, or teach English as a foreign language, or had experience of office or clerical work, particularly at management level, then list it. It could be the determining factor in getting the role-play company to pick out your CV and get you in front of them. I know two actors who were accountants. Obviously the high-living, Ferrari-driving, drug-fuelled world of accountancy all just became too much for them, and they decided to settle for the security of the acting world. Since then they've both spend a great deal of time as actors doing role-play about… accountancy.

Mark Shillabeer, a programme leader at Steps, says that they have a preference for a CV that highlights other corporate-work credits.

66 With the state of the market as it is we can be quite picky, and though lack of experience can be a problem, we are always looking for younger people. As well as corporate role-play experience, other examples of suitability can be examples of delivering good customer service. People who are fluent, and we mean fluent, in a second language can be very useful, and as Steps has expanded into areas such as India, Ghana, New Zealand and the USA, ethnic background is very important.

Debbie Manship at Role Call says that she likes to see an actor's credits as well as examples of corporate experience.

No one CV will cover all the needs. Try and do as much research as to what the company is looking for, and shape your CV accordingly.

For the purposes of keeping records, most companies will want an electronic copy of your CV and information, but it may well be worth on some occasions popping into their office and dropping off a hard copy. Try and judge it on a company-by-company basis. Don't use a 'one size fits all' approach.

You should try and make sure that your photograph is also suitable. The most glamorous of your ten-by-eights may not be the one that gets you an interview with the corporate company. Look at pictures of the people who work for the company on their website. In the case of the role-play companies, many of these people will be, or have been, actors. So avoid sending in the pictures in which you are heavy on lip gloss and dripping bling from each ear. This applies to actresses too!

Having sent out somewhere in the region of fifty to one hundred letters, there is a reasonable chance that one of these companies will reply and want to meet you.

Getting into Live-event Work

The corporate live-event companies are the ones least likely to call you in for a general meeting. If they do ask you to come in, it is probably because they have an event coming up and, from your letter and photograph, they think you might be suitable. This is another key reason why your photograph has to be a good and none-too-glamorous representation of what you actually look like: in other words, make sure you turn up for the meeting looking like the photograph!

It's not unknown for the live-event companies to cast actors from a photograph only. Many years ago when I started out in the corporate world, one of my first corporate gigs was for Lotus IBM. I was given the job with no interview and no meeting. A look at my photograph and a recommendation was all that happened. The job was an eight-minute short play, which was to be performed fourteen times a day at an exhibition in Birmingham NEC. Following this high point of artistic endeavour, there was a second play involving another actor: together we made up a twenty-minute show. Rehearsals, as always on these occasions, were minimal. A quick runthrough at the client's office, and then two late-night runthroughs on the company's stand the night before the exhibition opened. We hit the ground running on the Tuesday morning and performed for the whole day, alternating our two pieces.

As his show was my break, I didn't really get a chance to see the other actor in action, but it quickly became apparent to me that there was some sort of problem. The client felt he wasn't delivering exactly what they wanted. There was no one to direct him, and he was left to flounder. At the end of the day the client came to me and said: 'We're really happy with what you're doing, but we can't possibly have so-and-so (I genuinely can't remember the actor's name) on the stand again tomorrow.' The result was that this nameless actor was fired there and then and sent home. I rang an actor I knew who is an extremely fast learner and very reliable. He arrived in Birmingham at 10.30 p.m. that evening and we sat up in the hotel room until 2.00 a.m. going through his lines. Then, with the aid of some carefully placed crib sheets on his desk, he gave his first performance at 10.30 a.m. the following morning and never looked back.

The main point here is that many people in the corporate production companies don't really know how to cast. The actor concerned hadn't done anything wrong, and would probably be good in the right role and with the right support. Simply casting him from his photograph had put him in a situation where he wasn't able to work at his best.

Your photograph will be of prime importance to the client and production company alike. Similarly, being honest on your CV is also incredibly important in these situations. If you've written down basic fire-eating as one of your skills, then my goodness, you'd better be able to do it, as it's more than likely you'll find yourself standing in front of an audience of five hundred with two flaming torches in your hand before you can say: 'But I only do Shakespeare!'

As I've explained, many of the corporate live-event companies don't recruit their actors through agents, although they will sometimes circulate job details on casting services such as Castweb or the Equity Job Information Service. It's worth monitoring both these sources if you can, as the person at the other end of the request at the event company will be absolutely fine about receiving CVs from actors as well as from agents.

Just make sure that you are ideally suited to whatever they are asking. Actors do have a tendency, and I speak from experience in my younger years, to think that they can play anything and everything. One of the ways to become successful in the corporate world is to find your niche and stick to it. If they're asking for a 6' blond male, don't apply if you are 5'10" with light-brown hair. It means your CV will be disregarded, and perhaps the next time they put out a job they will remember your name or your photo and won't call you in as they think of you as a time-waster, even though, this time, you may actually have been suitable.

At an interview for a corporate job, do have your questions prepared. You should find out exactly what the job entails:

- Just how much rehearsal will there be?
- How much dialogue is there to learn?
- How many shows in the day?

Ask the questions with a good grace, but make sure you have as full a picture as possible as to what will be asked of you.

Getting into Role-play Work

The role-play company auditions tend to be more recognisable as a format that you will have endured before.

Some of the smaller role-play companies just ask you to come in for a meeting. They may run a trial role-play with you, but many of them feel that actually getting to know you and speaking to you is probably the most important thing.

The larger companies like Steps have audition days. These are half-day workshops where they will ask a group of people to come in and they will take them through one of the forms of role-playing that I've outlined earlier in the book.

If you have studied the chapters on role-play then nothing that happens on these days should come as a surprise. Remember, they are looking for potential, not necessarily the finished product. Don't feel that you have to go in there demonstrating just how much you know about the process.

Each role-play company has adapted the types of role-playing (bespoke, pre-briefed and Forum Theatre) to suit themselves, and they will all want you to perform them in a slightly different way.

Mark Shillabeer at Steps once again:

" If we like people from their CV and letter, we will bring them in for a workshop. Typically eight to fourteen people join us for a half-day workshop, and we would expect each of them to do a one-to-one role-play situation. We'd also test their feedback and facilitation skills and get them to do a simple Forum Theatre. We tend to follow these workshops up with a letter to people saying that we feel they could be a useful role-player for Steps. That doesn't, however, mean that we're going to be on the phone straight away with a job. It's just the start.

Prepare yourself for the meeting. Look up the company's website. Look at the clients they have worked with. Are there are any actors you know who have worked with that company?

Although essentially all these companies provide the same services, they all provide them in a slightly different way. Steps are very different from Role Call; Interact have their own methods, which are different in turn from React.

Ask the company what the process is after the audition. You may be very familiar from your more mainstream work with going to castings and interviews and then never hearing anything about it. Which is how you learn that you didn't get the job. This is not normal practice in the business sector where people do respond with a 'no' as well as a 'yes'.

If you've been to several role-play company auditions and don't seem to be hitting the mark, then it would not be unreasonable to ask for some feedback: 'What was it about me that you felt stopped me from being suitable?' It may be something you can change. It may not. It is certainly worth finding out.

The Business Plan: Objectives

Remember you are working on this as a business plan. Note down the audition, what happened, and any feedback you received.

By now your business plan document should be extending to several pages. Some of the leads you initially found may have turned into auditions or meetings. You have kept a record of this, and now you're just waiting for one of these to turn into a job.

Set yourself reasonable objectives. It's not very realistic to expect to read this book on a Monday, decide to become a corporate actor on the Tuesday, send out some letters on the Wednesday, get an interview on Thursday, and complete the job by the end of Friday.

If you think back to the chapter where we talked about setting up a bespoke role-play, reference was made to the use of smart objectives:

S   specific

M   measurable

A   attainable

R   relevant

T   timed

That is exactly what the objectives in your plan to become a corporate actor have to be.

Specific

Are you hoping to work in role-playing? Are you hoping to work in live events? Do you feel you would be better suited to working in training?

Measurable

Set out the objectives little by little so you always know where you are. For example: 'I will write fifty letters by Wednesday.' Then by the end of Wednesday it is possible to measure exactly where you are in terms of your objectives.

Attainable

It might be possible to write the letters by the end of Wednesday, or it might not. You are the best judge of how fast you work. If you want to set yourself an objective of five contacts today, then that might be easily attainable. You might want to set yourself a higher target, but whatever you choose, you should set something that you feel you can manage, otherwise you will start to fail. And feeling you have failed is not good.

Relevant

You are aware that, as an actor with little or no experience in the corporate market, the amount of work you're going to gain in it immediately is not going to be huge. Having decided to become a corporate actor and focus on corporate work, it's hardly realistic to have an objective of completing ten corporate jobs by the end of the following month.

Timed

Most important of all, set out this work plan with a timescale. Include everything from research, sending emails, following up the emails, attending interviews, and buying suitable clothes if need be.

Once these objectives are set into your strategy, you can create a step-by-step plan for yourself that becomes much easier to follow.

Keeping Your Agent Happy

There are other things you should consider in this process while you are applying for jobs, or hopefully shortly after you have been offered one.

Have that chat with your agent. Explain that you intend to focus on getting yourself at least four to five days of corporate work each month. Ask them how they would like you to manage your availability. Some agents like you to be able to send in your availability at the beginning of the month and stick to it.

I have a spreadsheet template on my computer for the month. Somewhere around the 16th of the month I will fill in jobs that have come in for the following month onto the spreadsheet. I colour-code them. Any jobs I know I cannot cancel – for instance, because they involve foreign travel and the plane tickets have been booked, or because I have committed that I will deliver the job for the client and no one else – these jobs I mark in purple.

Other jobs booked in are marked in yellow and I attach a note at the bottom of the sheet saying that any jobs marked in this colour are available for change if I get at least forty-eight hours' notice. It is then my decision whether to cancel this job for a casting interview or not.

This also ensures that my agent doesn't put me up for jobs that are filming on days when I am already committed. As and when other jobs come in, I update this sheet and send it to my agent on an ongoing basis, until the middle of the next month when I send a new availability sheet for the next six weeks.

The main thing here is to maintain a dialogue. The fact that I am self-sufficient allows both of us to give my career a little time to breathe so that as and when jobs come up, she can immediately check whether I'm free and suggest me for the job. And it means that she isn't wracked with guilt at the thought of me sitting at home with barely two baked potatoes to rub together because she has not got me an interview and an enormous fee from BBC *Doctors*.

Ask your agent how they feel about you doing role-play work. As I have already said, most agents would probably prefer you to be doing something that uses your skills and keeps you ready for work.

If you are chasing this work yourself, you may feel there is no reason that you should pay commission on the work to your agent. This has to be something that you and your agent come to an agreement about.

As I have said earlier, it would seem logical that, if you are finding this work for yourself, then you should not have to pay commission on it. The agent, however, may start to lose some work or not be able to put you up for jobs because of your commitment to role-play and corporate. It's a delicate balance.

One of the things that putting the work through your agent can help with is the fact that your agent's accounts department will do all the invoicing, etc., for you. If not, you will be responsible for producing an invoice for each job to be sent to the production company after the event.

Invoicing, Expenses and Cashflow

These companies deal with hundreds of invoices each week. They will expect to see something professional, clear, easy to read and with all the relevant detail on it. In return, you don't want to have to be constantly supplying them with further information and delaying your payment.

Most corporate production companies and role-play companies tend to pay on one of two systems: either thirty days from the date of the invoice, or at the end of the month following the month when the invoice was sent in, e.g. sending in an invoice on 9th May means you will be paid on 30th June.

You should take these delays in payment into your calculations and your plan.

You will be expected to pay the expenses of the job up front. This can include train and Tube fare, and taxis from the local station to the venue. Keep the receipts. You will be expected to submit a scan of all receipts with your invoice. Some companies will only accept the original receipts, which is a little annoying as this now means you have to send in the invoice by post rather than emailing it.

Train receipts are easy enough to get. For travel across London, most companies want to see a printout of your Oyster card for the date concerned, so make sure you register the card and can manage it online. This will enable you to get a printout to submit with your invoice. If you're driving by car, make sure you have agreed the mileage allowance before the journey, and whether you need a petrol receipt to back this up. Check.

You are now moving in a business and corporate world. You need to behave in a way they expect you to. Production companies and role-play companies alike will thank you for prompt submission of invoices. In many cases they themselves can't invoice the client until they have collected all the invoices and receipts from the actors on the job. So if one actor doesn't invoice for nearly three weeks – and this has been known to happen – three weeks are added on to the time that all the other people on the job have to wait before getting paid.

You can use the opportunity of emailing your invoice to the company to say a quick thank-you for the job. This helps prolong the dialogue between yourself and the account managers in the role-play companies who are selecting people for work.

Keep it businesslike. Personally I'd steer away from such comments as 'and I have lots of availability coming up so I'd really really love to do something for you soon'. Much more effective is to include a brief note such as 'Please find my invoice attached for the job on 3rd March. The client seemed happy, and all seemed to go well. Many thanks for thinking of me.' Make this personal but keep it to the point.

Feedback

The clients give feedback to the role-play companies. In my experience a lot has to go wrong for a client to feed back that they don't want an actor on a particular job any more, but it does happen.

Once when working on a long-term job for a large media company, I had to provide a team of ten role-players. On the second day, two of the strongest female role-players that I know went in to do the job, but at the end of the day I received a call from the client to say that he didn't think they were a good fit. The course had been a difficult day with tricky participants and things just had not worked out.

Sometimes people don't like people.

There's nothing you can do about that, but as long as you ensure that you turn up for the job well prepared, having read all the briefs, on time, looking smart, and prepared to listen to instructions from and work with the facilitator, then there should be no problem.

When you get back home, make a note on your business plan or in a notebook as to who the facilitator was you worked with that day. Make a note of anything special about how they liked to run the session. Add any feedback they gave you, or anything that will help you work smoothly with them a second time.

Many facilitators build up relationships with particular actors, and some will ask role-play companies for specific people if they are available. The role-play companies will always say they cannot guarantee the provision of a particular actor due to work commitments, but the client is king, and if that actor is in fact available then it would be a foolish role-play company that doesn't provide him or her.

Moving On

So hopefully by now, having followed this plan, you will have achieved your target, if it was a realistic one, of having completed a corporate job. If, having auditioned for the role-play companies, you find you are unsuccessful, then rethink. Perhaps you should be contacting some companies who do live events. What other special skills do you have that you could sell to them? You might like to look at promotional and logistics work and contact the agencies who use actors for that. Whatever happens, keep that record, keep those targets, and treat it as a business.

There are a large number of actors who now work entirely in the corporate market. In order to maximise their income and their opportunities in this field, some no longer have agents to look for film, television and theatre work. You might find this a difficult decision – to give up what your initial dream of acting was all about – but there are stages in life where other pressures make us change our choices. The idea that, by maintaining contact with role-playing training companies, by searching out the live-event work and by getting a reputation for being good at it, you can earn a significant income may suddenly become more attractive as you settle down with your mortgage or begin to think about starting a family.

Even if you don't give up on film, television and theatre, a couple of days' corporate work a month can be the difference between surviving through your twenties as a young actor, or giving up at the age of twenty-five and fast-tracking into a job with the Home Office.

Actors often have very little choice in their career. They often have to wait at the will of others for decisions to be made that will affect their future. When those decisions don't go in your favour, it can make you feel unwanted, undervalued and helpless. Moving into the corporate world doesn't necessarily change this, but it can allow you to have more control over your work, and structure your career. It can allow you to chase work more proactively rather than waiting for people to call you. It can help give you a sense of fulfilment in that you're using the skills you acquired in your actor training to help others.

And there may be one of you, just one of you, who reads this book, takes in all the information about the current opportunities available to actors in the corporate market, and ignores it all… to come up with the next big idea for using actors and skills.

I can't tell you what that will be as you haven't thought of it… yet!

Survey Results

This is a very quick snapshot of some of the questions I asked actors and agents doing research for this book.

The survey for actors was circulated using social media, mainly through The Actors Centre in Covent Garden, and 171 responses were received.

The survey for agents was circulated through the casting service Castweb and a total of 41 responses were received.

Actors

1. Have you ever done any corporate work as an actor?

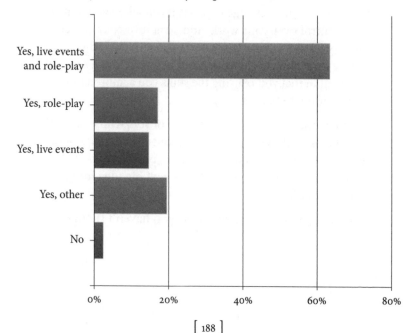

2. Did you train at a drama school and, if so, when did you graduate?

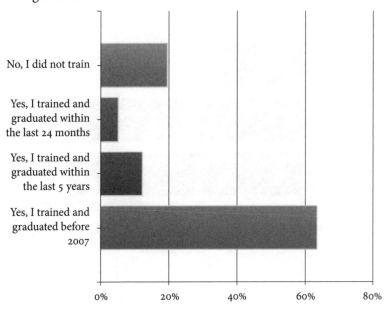

3. Did your training include any reference to corporate work?

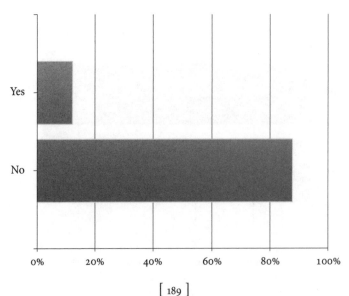

4. How did you get you corporate work?

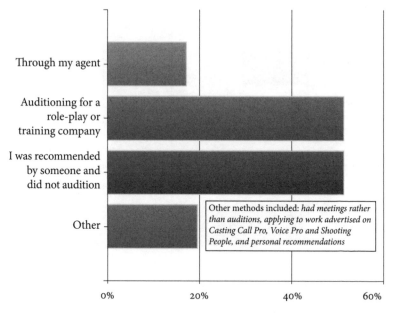

Other methods included: *had meetings rather than auditions, applying to work advertised on Casting Call Pro, Voice Pro and Shooting People, and personal recommendations*

5. Do you feel that a corporate job is a 'proper job'?

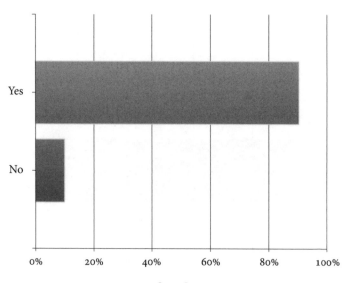

6. Did you feel that the job was well paid?

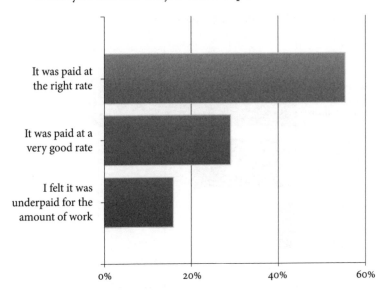

7. Did you feel that you were prepared for the job in terms of training?

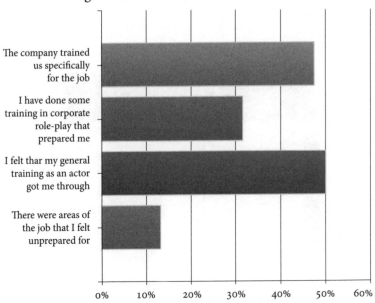

Agents

1. Do you put clients up for corporate work?

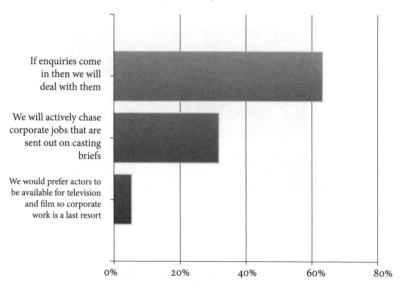

2. Do you have actors who, to your knowledge, do role-play work?

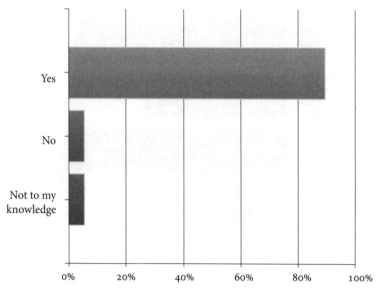

3. Would you expect to take commission on this work?

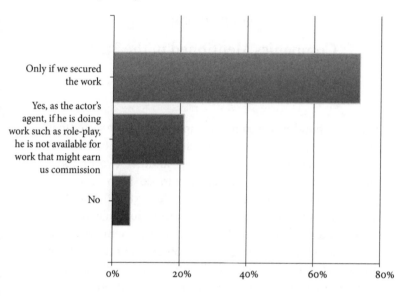

4. Would you price an actor higher for a corporate enquiry rather than for an enquiry from more mainstream work?

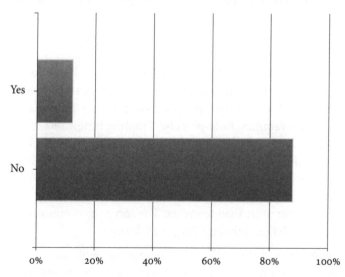

APPENDIX B

Companies Mentioned in the Text

There are hundreds of companies in the corporate sector that use actors. To list them all would turn this book into a reference manual and take at least another two or three hundred pages. What I've chosen to do is to allow the companies that I have mentioned in the text of the book to write a short paragraph about themselves. Hopefully this will give you a guide on how best to approach them and what they're looking for. There are many other books that you can use as well as the internet to build up a database of corporate companies. *Contacts* has a list of role-play companies and is published by Spotlight. *The White Book* is a reference work used by corporate-event companies themselves and lists many events companies and suppliers in the corporate world.

RPfT – Role-plays for Training

Role-plays for Training was started in 1988 when a local-government-housing-officer-turned-actor was asked to help source actors for the purpose of training advisers to homeless families. Role-plays for Training is now one of the longest established role-play companies in the UK. This successful company has an emphasis on offering excellent service and working ethically with actors, trainers and clients alike. Many of our clients have been using our services for more than ten years. The company is now run by Adrian McLoughlin and Fergus Mclarnon.

We have a very large client list in both the public sector and private sector. We work now on a global basis. Increasingly we need actors who are highly skilled facilitators. They must have a good grasp of training models and be able to run whole days either as the support facilitator or the lead facilitator.

Always call before sending a CV as it saves time. We only actively recruit once a year at most.

www.roleplaysfortraining.co.uk

Steps

A global leader in experiential drama-based training since 1992, Steps specialises in developing facilitated, interactive training and innovative learning solutions that inspire people to act differently. We work with clients across all sectors, designing and delivering bespoke training and development programmes covering topics including diversity and inclusion, leadership, performance management, customer service and personal impact. Our unique approach brings to life situations where behaviour creates challenges for individuals, teams and businesses. Using a variety of interactive techniques, including role-play (one-to-one skills practice) and Forum Theatre (a collective experience giving participants a chance to alter the course of the action), our associates are adept at portraying 'as real' characters and situations – complemented by expertise in facilitation and sensitive feedback skills. We have over one hundred and twenty actor/facilitators based across the UK and internationally, speaking over twenty world languages, and we believe that our relationship with them really sets us apart – in terms of the calibre of the associates we attract and the service they help us provide to our clients. We often source actor/facilitators to meet client needs – be that a language requirement, a geographic location or a particular cultural demographic – and the diversity of our associate base is something we are very proud of. If you are interested in joining the *Steps* team, please visit our website for details of how to submit a CV and headshot.

www.stepsdrama.com.

Role Call

After a successful career as an actress, including several television series (*Angels, Dr Who, The District Nurse*), Debbie Manship established Role Call in 1989 as a training consultancy specialising in providing role-players and facilitators for training courses within both public and private sectors. Role Call's clients include HMRC, AstraZeneca, The Cabinet Office, Allen and Overy and Deutsche Bank, for whom Role Call has provided everything from management development courses through to live-event productions.

Role Call also has more than twenty years' experience working with health professionals at all levels and disciplines. Debbie and her team at Role Call work all over Europe within courses covering general communication skills, breaking bad news, informed consent, etc., and an enormous variety of doctor–patient scenarios. Role Call works with many of the major teaching hospitals throughout the UK and organisations such as Cancer Research UK, The Kings Fund and several of the Royal Colleges.

Debbie's most recent projects for pharmeceutical companies include the following scripts for Conferences and DVD productions: 'Could Do Better, Must Try Harder' (ADHD) and 'Home & Dry' (Urge Incontinence) for UCB, and 'Breathe' (Multiple Myeloma) for Johnson and Johnson. Role Call has also produced and directed several facilitator-training DVDs for the National Cancer Action Team.

For the last several years, Debbie has focused particularly on scriptwriting and creating and facilitating group and individual training and development programmes.

Contact by email only please: debbie@rolecall.co.uk

Kru Live

Founded in 2005, Kru Live is a specialist staffing and implementation agency that carries out the majority of its work for experiential, public-relations and event agencies that do not have in-house staffing departments. Following many years' experience working for staffing and experiential agencies and carrying out a market analysis and research study into the effect and importance of team selection on brand value, Kru Live's founder Tom Eatenton set about the task of creating a staffing agency to address the key failings he had noticed in the supply of staff in the industry and to deliver a service of excellence not only to clients but to their staff, those that make the difference between an 'okay' campaign and a 'fantastic' campaign.

Thorough and detailed briefings and adequate, timely and fair pay systems, the ability to feed back thoughts, ideas and improvements and regular communication are the things that we, and the best field staff in the industry, feel are what makes a specialist agency stand out from the rest.

We have created an agency that specialises in the provision of outsourced implementation and staffing services for clients with their own specialisms. Our clients have confidence in our ability and discretion because we have a track record of success and do not offer services to brands or agencies on a creative level. We focus solely on delivering staffing, campaign management and peripheral services and so can never be seen as 'competition'. We are held in high regard by our clients because, like them, we stick to what we know best.

FMBE Award Winner in the 'Staffing Agency of Year' category.

Actors wanting to apply for work should visit the website at www.krulive.com or email register@krulive.com for more information.

APPENDIX

Jillie Bushell Associates

Jillie Bushell Associates was established over twenty years ago. After a long and successful career as a performer herself, Jillie Bushell created the company after several years working 'in-house', running the Entertainment and Speaker Division for Purchase Point, one of the most prominent corporate production agencies of its time. Whilst there, she engaged many actors for video and live-action (role-play) scenarios and played a leading role in developing the popularity of this genre.

Now this diverse Music, Speaker and Entertainment Agency goes from strength to strength, and has worked on some of the world's largest and most prestigious events. Their reputation amongst clients, artists and speakers alike, as one of the most prominent players in the industry, is a great source of pride for Jillie. Their ability to provide a complete 'end to end' service, managing Artists' and Speakers' logistics and working as part of the event team on-site, make the company a unique proposition, supplying only the best and most established performers and services.

www.jilliebushell.com

Twisted Events Presents

Ben Cooper and Janet Rawson set up Twisted Events Presents in 2009. Their combined professional backgrounds cover producing, directing, acting and writing for theatre, arts and the media. They produce tailor-made, professional theatrical events to bring fun and sparkle to the thoughts, themes and ideas of their clients.

They are a UK-wide theatrical-events company, building a reputation for designing exciting, diverse, bespoke events, productions and team-dynamic days.

www.twistedeventspresents.co.uk

www.nickhernbooks.co.uk

facebook.com/nickhernbooks

twitter.com/nickhernbooks